FROM ARROGANCE TO INTIMACY

A Handbook for Active Democracies

Andy Williamson & Martin Sande

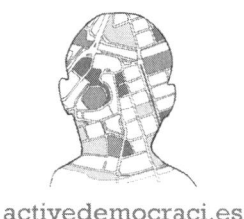

activedemocraci.es

FROM ARROGANCE TO INTIMACY: A HANDBOOK FOR ACTIVE DEMOCRACIES

Andy Williamson & Martin Sande
First edition published 2014

Active Democracies is a Democratise & Co-Lab by Preera Co-production.
London & Gothenburg

For more information contact us at **info@activedemocraci.es**, visit **activedemocraci.es** or **facebook.com/activedemocracies**

Cover design by sventheelk.com

ISBN 978-1-326-00460-6

Foreword

It is an honour for me to write the foreword to Andy and Martin's new book. Along with my colleagues, Anders Nordh and Kjell-Åke Eriksson, I can take some credit for making this book possible. Why you may wonder? Because it was at the Swedish Association of Local Authorities and Regions (SALAR) eDemocracy summit that Martin and Andy got to know each other. This was in the spring of 2012, where we invited experts from different countries to come together to share and learn about developments in citizen engagement around the world and to identify what was going to be required of the Swedish municipalities and counties in the near future.

So it was there that Martin and Andy found each other. They began to think about what is needed to make democracy better and what they could do to ignite this fire. They want to help us to make changes in the kind of democratic systems we have in the western world. After all, the experts at our 'Summit' told us clearly that we have problems! We have problems with trust, with legitimacy, alienation and inequality. We have problems that are due to a lack of participation. And we have problems with the failure to modernise the established parties and with the increase in anti-democratic movements.

It has now been two years since that summit and this book is the result of those conversations, so I read "From arrogance to intimacy" with great curiosity. To create change some people must take the lead and dare to think differently. They must dare to provoke us so we start to feel uncomfortable with our present situation and challenge us to create something new. We need people to "rock the boat" in our democracies. To challenge the rest of us to accept our individual responsibilities to participate in the dialogue about what kind of society we want, to ask what are the values we want to be characterized by, what is required of me as a citizen and what is required of those who are the leaders in our democratic systems?

Martin and Andy possess the courage it takes to ignite this fire of change. Throughout this book, they offer us ways to help make our democracies better and encourage us to co-create with anyone who wants to engage in dialogue about the transformation of democracy. The dialogue they invite us into isn't one about who or what is right or wrong, it is about trying to understand our increasingly complex society. They want all of us to creatively explore different options and to give space to everyone so that they can contribute to an ongoing dialogue. Not least, they do this by inviting us all to contribute to future editions of this book.

Martin and Andy highlight the need for an active democracy. People have never been as dedicated to this idea as they are today, but many of them are doing it outside the traditional democratic process, not through the traditional parties and civil society organisations. Why is that? Is it because those traditional leaders are seen as arrogant? It is natural for new forms to replace the old, but is this happening because we are becoming more individualistic or even, perhaps, a more selfish society? Andy and Martin challenge my thinking in this book.

The book's starting point is to encourage us to move from arrogance to closeness, to intimacy. I know it's something the writers have thought a lot about and I think it is interesting for everyone to now be able to explore this with them and to see how they think the changes that they feel are needed in democracy can start to happen.

Their analysis of why citizens have become "disconnected" from democracy is an important basis for further dialogue. Is it that the New Public Management model introduced widely since the 1990s has influenced the development of society and people's relationship to government and the bigger public? Where we are increasingly seen as customers and not citizens, we are looking for individual satisfaction and not for the wider public benefit. How does this affect our democracy? Who listens to the public and who speaks for whom? Do you make it convenient for them or just listen to your peers? How do the agendas of think tanks and others actually influence decisions and what issues are raised when they have a lack of transparency? Is that a working democracy? How will the incredible digital developments we have seen in recent decades impact? Though many are very positive there are also darker sides.

The digital revolution and its potential has been given its very own section in the book. Andy has long worked around the world with digitization and its role in democracy, participation and commitment. What we can see is that many public agencies use digital channels without really having thought through why and how. Andy and Martin's thoughts and advice on this are an opportunity to look at our own approaches to using digital media. These digital channels are providing unprecedented opportunity to co-create together with citizens. Where this is done properly, it's about the important issues and a real desire to achieve results, but one must also take into account its limitations.

Transformation is a term that occurs more and more when we talk about the need for social change and movement. Transformation requires a vision of the future, how we want society to look, what the movement is that we want to accomplish. An increasingly complex society requires co-creation, both in developing the scenario and to provide movement. Martin and Andy highlight several key components to facilitate the emergence of transformation. This is all about what you and I can do as individuals, but it is primarily about the word "we": how can we, together, in our different roles create a sustainable democratic, social, economic, ecological society for ourselves and future generations.

In the book's final section, Martin and Andy's ideas about how we move forward to a more active democracy are developed. In this, local government, its elected representatives and officials, take on a leading role but not to have power over others rather to share power. This in turn can create greater legitimacy for and develop our democratic systems and ensure sustainable development.

I have read the book with great interest and would like to participate in the ongoing dialogue about the development of democracy. I am convinced that since you are holding the book in your hand you now will read it with interest. You might not agree with everything in it but I am sure you will find it interesting and that there is something for you to contribute.

Finally, thanks to Martin and Andy for taking the first steps to start the fire and to begin the dialogue about how we develop democracy in our rapidly changing and increasingly complex society.

Lena Langlet
Head of Citizen Involvement and Democracy
Swedish Association of Local Authorities and Regions

Acknowledgements

This book is the result of many conversations. It's going to be impossible to thank everyone who has contributed to our thinking. So, we're just going to list a few, with our apologies to those we miss out and an invitation to others to think about becoming part of the conversation going forward. Above all we'd both like to thank Lena Langlet, Anders Nordh, Kjell-Åke Eriksson, Christine Feuk and many others at the Swedish Association of Local Authorities and Regions (SALAR), they have been central to our thinking and our work. We've also been inspired and motivated by our colleagues who participated in SALAR's e-Participation and Democracy Summits. We'd like to thank our clients, who have inspired us, allowed us to develop our ideas, helped us validate them and accepted that the world is always in beta.

Andy: I want to thank Esther Foreman for her insights, support and friendship. Anthony Zacharzewski, Alistair Stoddart and others at the Democratic Society, Edward Andersson and Catherine Howe have played a part in the evolution of my thinking for this book. Mike Gurstein, Peter Day, Steve Thompson and Larry Stillman have been friends and colleagues for a long time and I've learned much from them. In the parliamentary realm, John Pullinger (UK House of Commons), Moira Fraser (New Zealand Parliament), Roxanne Missingham (Australian Parliament), Soledad Ferreiro (Biblioteca del Congreso Nacional de Chile), Ellie Valentine (Ukraine Parliament), Andy Richardson (Inter-parliamentary Union) and Gherardo Casini (Global Centre for ICT in Parliament) stand out as having helped shape my ideas, as have Tiago Piexoto (World Bank), Morten Meyerhoff

Nielsen (Danish Government), Simon Burall (Involve), Ingrid Prikken (OPM), Paul Evans and Clifford Singer elsewhere. There are many others.

My journey started in Aotearoa New Zealand, so I want to acknowledge and thank the Waitakere whanau for showing me how community really works, not least Greg Presland, Bob Harvey, Penny Hulse and David Cunliffe. This book is in many ways a journey from Laingholm, on the shores of the Manukau Harbour, to Långholmen in central Stockholm.

Finally, it goes without saying that I need to thank Martin for being both friend and colleague on this inspiring and powerful journey. I need to thank Julie Melrose for listening to an interminable torrent of sometimes random and often crazy ideas, reading drafts and making cups of tea. And I want to dedicate this book to my boys, Matthew, Evan and Reuben because they are why all this matters.

Martin: First of all, none of my work would have been possible without the courage and conviction of SALAR. Their desire to co-create and shift both thinking and action is very real and courageous. I cannot express how proud I feel being trusted by them and given the opportunity and space to act and co-create. Thank you to municipalities and regions of Sweden who have been involved in breaking new ground. I hope that I have been able to be respectful and to live up to your expectations.

Andy, my friend and co-colleague, my warmest thanks and gratitude for your openness, energy and clarity. It seems when we met in 2012 we were searching in the same direction, just coming from different paths of life. Now we can walk side by side to make a real difference and an impact in our shared societies.

Learning and evolving within complexity is a lifelong adventure, I am privileged to have guides who help me find my way and co-create shared paths. Special thanks to these guides for creating clarity and sharing their passion: Hans Abrahamsson at Göteborg University, Bernard LeRoux from The City of Gothenburg, Tor Eneroth from BVC, Navid Modiri from everywhere, Myrna Lewis of Deep Democracy in South Africa for helping me to see the value of 'no' and Per Bergström for having such energy for a better future.

My work in democracy and societal issues has been enabled by incredible people, daring and caring about ideas that initially might be seen as at best odd and sometimes purely crazy. Clients sharing a passion to co-create new ways and the courage to try them in practice involve thousands of people over the years. All the Mayors, like Lena Facht, and CEOs, like Tord Linder and Nils Andreasson, in the early learning days of the late 1990s deserve a special thanks for their courage and belief in an energetic and naive young man and his colleagues at Preera. Preera is a special place with special people, we share a deep desire to make a difference and this is truly engrained in our culture. Not always easy, yet always meaningful to pursue. I am proud to be a part of the energy that team Preera creates every day with our clients and with each other. The Transformation Alliance shares this energy so a great thanks to colleagues in France, Italy and Germany.

And, of course, I want to thank my family, Eva, Emma and Matilda. You give me perspectives of who I am and when I lose track of my direction and energy. Each of you have a special ability for making me grateful every day to be alive. Thank you.

Table of Contents

A FRAMEWORK FOR TRANSFORMATION

ROAD MAP FOR ACTIVE DEMOCRACIES

INVITATION TO CO-CREATION

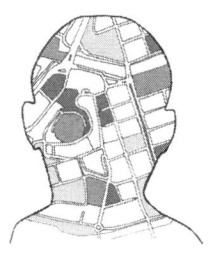

Introduction

You Are Here

We have a problem. Too many of us feel that democracy is broken. Too many of us distrust our politicians, despair at the rise of bureaucracy and feel ignored when it comes to the decisions that affect our lives. These are the same lives that have changed beyond recognition over the last 50 years (and especially the last 10). Thanks to digital and social tools we are now more connected than at any time in human history and yet we often feel more isolated and lost than ever before. We have replaced community with light connections. And despite the constancy of change some things have failed to keep pace. Our systems of governance and representation, for example, feel like they have hardly moved. As our lives and our societies have become faster, more complex, more open and more challenging, democracy appears stubbornly rooted in the past. It remains largely impervious to the changes around it.

Democracy has become a giant project in which shadowy actors seek to manage and control. Not just politicians and civil servants but lobbyists, public affairs and corporate agendas. Far from being a liberator and igniter of community action, democracy all too often feels restrictive, drawing us towards a dulled-down normative state of inaction and compliance. Our democracies are too complex. So complex few of us really know how they work. Too complex to have been designed, this is not some giant conspiracy theory just a dysfunctional ecosystem. Our democracies have evolved over time to be closed and opaque. They have evolved to privilege some of us (the few) over others (the many) and they have become exclusive and excluding. Even where this is not through intent, it has happened through presumed practicality. And it is wrong.

Our democracies rarely reflect the communities that they are supposed to help. Put bluntly, our democratic systems have become arrogant and controlling. This cannot continue. Many of us are questioning the status quo and increasingly citizens are refusing to accept things as they are. Right around the world people are refusing to accept closed, opaque, slow and sly democracy. And let's be clear, the challenge is not when but how we are going to change.

Our current democratic systems often appear as out of balance hierarchies: representatives at the top, the public at the bottom with various intermediaries in between. Some of these intermediaries are connectors, some are blockers. Many people don't like this because they sense an inherent unfairness. Some people pretend they don't like it, but in reality it suits them because hierarchies are about power – hierarchies are arrogant and controlling and "there needs to be a significant rebalancing of power".[1]

We believe it's time to start thinking differently, to reframe democracy and we have the opportunity to do this together. To start seeing society as a network and democratic representation happening in the context of this network. This networked democracy lets us focus on mutuality, trust and co-creation. It allows us to see the system and those who represent us in that system as part of our network. When we do, we can start to become intimate and co-creating. And where we do we create the intention to shift power so it's used 'with' and not 'against'; for the benefit of all not the privilege of the few.

This book is our attempt to start the shift away from arrogance towards intimacy. It started as a conversation and we hope it will help

---

[1] The Power Inquiry. (2006). Power to the people. York: Joseph Rowntree Charitable Trust & Joseph Rowntree Reform Trust.

start some more conversations. We hope that it will play a small part in helping us to shape a better democratic future. But we have to caution you that this is not a book about simple solutions. The problem is too complex for that. Nor do we believe that we have all the answers. That would be arrogant. All we have to offer are our shared experiences and perspectives. We also have a lot of questions to ask you and some ideas that, we hope, will help stimulate your thinking and our shared actions. We want to help you challenge current assumptions about how democracy works and start to rebuild a new, more inclusive democracy.

This book is about igniting change. We believe that it's the small incendiary changes that, when brought together, can re-shape governance, democracy and representation into something we recognise as being a valid, valuable and trusted part of our networked age. But it can't really be a 'how to' guide to better democracy either. Democracy is too nuanced, far too contextual. It is too rich for that to be possible. So on a practical level we hope it will start you thinking, exploring and accelerating your ideas as you start to co-design a new democracy to meet your community's future needs (with the emphasis on the personal and communal – on the local).

Before we can do this, we need to break democracy down to its basic elements, into a number of constituent parts. Most obvious is the part where citizens are engaged in some form of consultation but this is an action point surrounded by both internal (governmental) process and by external civic action. Less obvious but equally important are the cultural and organisational processes that support or inhibit access, accessibility and engagement. Again these exist not only inside our institutions but within and between all the different actors, including within the architecture of the digital networks that we take for granted but which are vulnerable to control and manipulation. So, this is a book about process: an emergent process. It's a book about vision. This is why we want to partner with you to co-create new ways of doing democracy. And above all it's not a book for the radicals, the political anoraks and geeks, the anarchists or the extreme. It's a book for everyone, those on the inside as much as those on the outside. Our point: democracy is everyone's responsibility and to co-create a system that works we need everyone involved.

It's time to take you from this old world of arrogance and control to a new one of intimacy and co-creation! We've created this book because we believe change is needed. We hope we can (in a small way at least) inspire, lead, guide and support you, your organisation, your community and the people around you on a journey from outmoded ways of decision making to ones that support dynamic, organic and pro-social ways of connecting, conversing and deciding.

This is a process, not an event. And, as we'll see, the journey to active democracies is long overdue. We have come to a critical moment in time where we need to re-invent what we mean by democracy, when we have to re-think the processes that make our society function. Otherwise we're simply dinosaurs staring at an approaching comet.

The journey matters. And, like all journeys, re-building democracy is going to have highs and lows, problems and opportunities. There are challenges and hopefully some golden moments. Above all there is the potential for transformation and learning to come from these pages. This is a learning journey, an explorative one with no fixed destination, just a lot of history, a lot of chances to stop, reflect, and to innovate. Hopefully it's a journey that comes with passion and energy to do stuff better. And above all it will come with personal as well as organisational and systemic transformation.

Because every step you take is a place to learn.

Why Write This Book?

This book is the result of a collection of conversations. Conversations the authors have had together and with a lot of like-minded people around the world. People, like us, who realise that something has to change. Not just activists and campaigners, these conversations include ordinary people, public servants at all levels, members of parliaments and councillors. In other words, people at every level of society who all bring their unique experiences, knowledge and opinions of representative democracy but who all feel things have to change.

We've written this book because we've worked in the democratic sector for long enough to know there's a problem. One question we are asked over and over is 'how can we bring about change?' How can things change when there is so much resistance, so much power vested in the system and so much disconnection? Politicians tell us they feel trapped, civil servants say they don't know how to start the process of change and citizens turn away because they feel that the system isn't listening. So our conversations started with these questions and led us to write this book to understand the problems and start to explore alternatives. To explore what we have come to call 'active democracies'.

In May 2014, we co-facilitated a Democracy Summit, hosted by the Swedish Association of Local Authorities and Regions (SALAR)[2],

---

[2] See: www.skl.se

exploring with researchers, practitioners and professionals from Sweden, the UK, Germany, Iceland, Finland and Italy the challenges facing democracy. Independent of perspective or origin we all shared similar views on the challenges faced and insights needed about the actions that would make a difference. Re-engaging citizens in dialogue and debates, prototyping to learn, re-framing legitimacy and trust, grounded leadership and co-designing democracies all emerged as shared patterns in our collective work. A colleague, at another democratic event across the Baltic in Riga, was taken by the parallel process unfolding via Twitter: different groups, same issues. This book is a collection of conversations, at the 'Democracy Summit' a lot more people joined in and we invite you to join us and co-create the future too. In case it helps you understand where we're coming from, this is how we individually came to this place:

Martin: I bring a strong desire to make a difference and an energy for co-creation has been and will keep on being a strong motivation for me. Exploring new ways of thinking and acting and testing in new contexts has been a theme all my life. Mixing my time by working with my head and heart in processes involving large and small groups, to working with my hands cabinetmaking in wood, sewing fabrics and splicing ropes and wire for boats, and welding aluminium for one-off gear for boats. This passion drives me to be curious and to create. The learning comes out of pain and joy of trying; immersing myself into a field that is unknown and yet familiar enables many mistakes and successes to evolve into learning. For me every 'mistake' is a learning opportunity. I feel safe to fail, that's why I learn. Much thanks to my family, colleagues and employers and a deeply held belief that trying is always at the front of meeting a challenge.

Being a Master of Science from university in Sweden, in economics and management-control, I've learned and experimented with many models to improve organisations, and I've always doubted if it's the way to go. For me, recognising this deficit after only a couple of years in to my 'measurement-convicted career' I experienced the power of dialogue. I realised that there lies an enormous potential in co-creation through dialogue and participation. Since 1995 I have been co-experimenting practices to engage and establish new ways of co-creation in complex issues.

Since 2006 I've actively worked in Sweden through a close partnership with SALAR, seeking out and exploring ways to energise democracy through citizen dialogue and participation. The issues we're addressing are gaining in complexity, however, the fundamentals remain the same. Trust is built by dialogue and interaction. Complex issues require co-creation for viable answers to emerge and have the capacity to work in the real world. Resistance and alternative views always legitimately exist, so change cannot be pushed. It has to evolve and it has to create places for all voices to emerge.

In this work, we crossed paths and realised we share a desire to make a real difference for democracies. We were heading in the same direction, so we decided to walk together:

> If you want to walk fast, walk alone. If you want to walk far, walk together.

Andy: I started out my career in software development, moving into strategic consultancy and technology innovation, working with multi-nationals and start-ups. Always politically aware, I got increasingly involved in local and community politics in the late 1990s in Aotearoa New Zealand. A catalytic moment for me was realising that we (as a community) could use this new internet technology to unmask the incompetence, nepotism and out of control egos of dysfunctional politicians. So, we did. We took a critical report they were trying to embargo and bury and we published it. Six months later the council was re-elected and that party was wiped out. So from there I started doing more work both personally and professionally around digital

governance, engagement and democracy. I became Deputy Chair of
the New Zealand Government's Digital Strategy Advisory Group and I
was asked to Chair Waitakere Online, a council, community and
business partnership. I took up some academic study, and eventually
gained a PhD looking at how digital impacts on local democracy. This
work still informs a lot of what I do today because I quickly realised
that it was never about the technology but about people, processes
and culture. We have a saying in Aotearoa New Zealand:

He aha te mea nui o te ao?
He tangata! He tangata! He tangata![3]

Moving to the UK in 2007 my work shifted to focus much more on
engagement and working with parliaments. Since then I've worked
with, spoken at and given evidence and advice to many parliaments
and parliamentary fora, ranging from Australia, Canada, South Africa,
the UK and European Parliament to Peru, Serbia, Welsh Assembly and
the UAE – parliaments of all shapes, sizes and democratic maturity. In
all of them my message is clear; you've got to get out from the
institution. Open it up, engage people, listen a lot and make the whole
place more human, more accessible. Above all, governments and
parliaments need to become truly transparent and accountable.
Democracy has to become a networked eco-system. A place where we
can innovate and that means exploring, trying, doing, failing and lots
of learning. It's through my work with SALAR that I first met Marty.
We're both passionate about doing democracy better, about learning
and teaching what we know to help other people to do this. Where he
does this on the inside, I do it on the outside.

We: Our work together is about supporting people and organisations
to accept change as a constant, embrace this change and get excited
and engaged about the potential for creating new democratic futures

---

[3] What is the most important thing in the world? It is people! It is people! It is people!

together. This book is about bringing it all together! It was SALAR's 'e-Participation summit of 2012' that first brought us together. SALAR has energized and enabled innovative work on participation aimed at re-igniting local democracy in Sweden since SALAR's congress of 2006 initiated this committed and enduring work. Thanks to the foresight and curiosity of SALAR the authors' paths of work, innovative practice and ideas crossed and started intertwining. For that we are grateful.

You: What's your story? Do you want to share the journey with us?

How to Use This Book

We want to help you to create new solutions. First though we need to understand the deep-seated fundamental problems, otherwise our solutions will be shallow. So, we need a better map! For us, maps are important: GPS gives you directions, maps give you context! Maps are also subjective, they offer you alternatives because we're all coming from different places, taking different routes and seeing different things along the way. Democracy is not a 'one size fits all' experience!

We think it's important to introduce you to our concept of active democracies before we talk about the problems. This way you will have some context and an over-arching narrative for what we mean as the book progresses. It's in the third section that we will start to draw you a map of the present, situating ourselves properly in the world we are in now. Here we explain where we've come from, or looking at this in another way, how we got into this mess in the first place. We will explore five key reasons for disconnection (yes, we know there are many more!). Section four focusses exclusively on the digital agenda and how we use digital tools to enable networked democracy. We do this not because we want to idealise digital but because it offers us the greatest potential to create transformational and disruptive tools to support social change.

Recognising that digital is only a tool and that it's the social and cultural processes that really have to change if democracy is to work for all of us, in section five we introduce our framework for transformation. This is a set of stand-alone but inter-related concepts that together can enable active democracy. This is a set of macro conversations exploring concepts and ideas for transforming democratic culture. In section six we move on to present you with a roadmap for active democracies. This section contains some operational, hands-on things that you can start doing right away to transform democracy.

We're strong believers in praxis, applying theory to practice, and using practice to inform and refine theory. So we've not shied away from academic content where it's appropriate. However, this isn't an academic text, it's a practical book for people who want to make change happen.

Having said that, it's your journey, you can read it from beginning to end, dip in at random, choose the bits you like and ignore the bits you don't. If you want, just look at the pictures. As long as you learn something, that's OK.

This is not a normal book. You can re-use it. It's yours, take what we've written and add to it, change it, make it better. Write all over it. Use it to launch your own ideas. All we ask is that you acknowledge the original work and that, if you add, change or develop anything, please contribute back to the conversation by sharing it with us and others.

If you want to re-sell this book with your additions you can. You have our blessing but you're not allowed to do so for personal gain. All of the proceeds from this book go back into the Active Democracies project and we ask that you do the same. Talk to us to find out how!

Once you've read it, help us make it better. Become a co-author!

> ❖ Oh, and each chapter ends with a few quick 'takeaways' in a box like this.

A Co-creative Project

This book has been conceived as an agile project (as you'll see, we like the idea of using agile techniques for transforming democracy!). The version you're reading is in ~~alpha~~ beta and it will change. We've written it (or rather, we're writing it...) using lean methods and will continue to iterate new versions as conversations around active democracies emerge and are shared. The most essential work from now on will not be done by us alone. We have invited co-authors to collaborate and contribute by challenging, expanding and re-shaping our ideas and collecting conversations and capturing these in future editions of this book. We want everyone to share in the learning (well, we are trying to espouse principles of collaboration and co-creation!). And about the only thing we're sure of is that we don't have all the answers.

So we want to share some ideas, some of the things we've learned and describe some processes that we think might make a difference (that's this book in case you were wondering). But we also want you to tell us (and everyone else) your stories so that we can put some life into the ideas we share and together make them bigger and better.

So, let's just be clear. There are four key principles that inform our work and this book:

- control is over-rated;
- power used to create personal advantage will always fail;
- crowds are better at creating the future; and

- self-reflection helps us understand the impact of our actions.

We don't believe in control or holding onto power, we want to share what we know and encourage everyone reading this book to co-create a new democratic future with us. We believe that democracy – and particularly making democracy work better – is a journey rich in learning. Democracy by its very nature (Demos: the people) isn't a journey you can make alone.

If you share our vision for active democracies and would like to be part of the conversation and a co-author of the next edition then we invite you to join us.

You're reading an early edition and should consider it an invitation to co-create with us. We want to publish updated, collective revisions of the book over time. In between new editions, we hope that new and interesting stories will emerge and these and other resources will be available at the website for our shared network of co-creators.

Please visit us and get in touch at!

activedemocraci.es

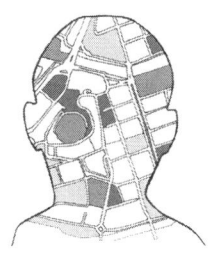

We Need Active Democracies

Situating Democracy

Our democracy is firmly locked in the past, it's based on past models and old ways of doing. Old ways of thinking. And it has many inherent problems: public disaffection with politics, economic crises, poverty, inequality, taxation, how to pay for an aging population, how to use that piece of waste land on the corner of your street. All too often intractable problems where assumptions are made, decisions are taken behind closed doors and people are left feeling angry, ignored and dis-enfranchised. We don't think this works and we see an urgent need to re-think democracy, to create an active democracy. So, to ground our ideas we want to briefly open the lid on some of the theory that lies behind this. Don't worry, we'll keep it brief! This chapter is important for us because it helps us frame active democracy and, hopefully, it will help you to understand where we're coming from too!

We're convinced that conversation lies at the heart of active democracy. Not any conversation, not the 'I am right, you are wrong' conversation we've all experienced, but authentic dialogue. That means dialogue which happens without hidden agendas or manipulation but with lots of active listening. Conversation. Discussion. Debate. Let's put these into shorthand and call them 'discourse', which philosopher Jurgen Habermas observed, doesn't happen on its own. In fact he suggests it must always be situated in the context of the public sphere in which it occurs. Discourse is neither random nor lacking context (even if this isn't always apparent). The public sphere is a place where debate occurs within our democratic process and somewhere that public opinion and publicity (even lobbying in a modern political context) occurs.[4] This is an ideal, not a given, and forces within the system are out to control the message, to 'colonise' it. It's very easy for us to look around and agree that public opinion has become "increasingly differentiated, specialised, institutionalised and professionalised".[5]

Look at the creeping technocracy of government as an example. They have become so concerned with the management of a process by a technical and political elite that, somewhere in the journey, the voices of ordinary people have been lost. Others use the example of lobbying and how it manipulates the message imposing undue, often opaque, influence from and for the benefit of those with money and power. In short, conversations are not created equally. It is naïve to think that today we all get a fair, some people want to control and manipulate the debate. These people are rarely acting in the best interests of the wider public.[6]

We should also lose the idea that there is one single public sphere, there are in fact many. Cunningham describes "specific spaces of self- and community-making and identity." He suggests that there is no ideal public sphere because our communication spaces are now so much more complex and saturated (has anyone looked at Facebook lately?). So, it's more appropriate, as Todd Gitlin argued, to consider the existence of fragmented sphericules of public space and opinion.[7] The internet accelerates this splintering even further. It's a rich communication media that has led to increased diversity, becoming a place where many smaller spheres are created and sustained (and

---

[4] Habermas, J. (1979). Communication and the evolution of society. Boston, MA: Beacon Press.

[5] Cunningham, S. (2000). Diasporic media and public 'sphericules'. Retrieved August 26, 2001, from www.nyu.edu/gsas/dept/media/pdfs/cunningham.pdf. p.3

[6] Gilens, M., Page, B.I. (2014). Testing theories of American politics: elites, interest groups, and average citizens. Perspectives on Politics (2014, Fall).

[7] Gitlin, T. (1998). Public sphere or public sphericules? In T. Liebes & J. Curran (Eds.), Media, ritual and identity (pp. 175-202). London: Routledge.

eventually fade and disappear). But adding new sphericules, such as those that occur online, is not necessarily a simple extension to public space. Indeed, Poster as far back as 1995 cautioned us not to accept the internet blindly as evolution or expansion, its network culture is different to traditional public spheres. And he was right, we have seen demonstrated over and over again that digital, and particularly social media, is as likely to lead to challenges of the status quo as to any acceptance or virtual extension of it.

For Habermas it is communication that mediates the public sphere, and, for the sake of this discussion, sphericules.[8] And notwithstanding the comments above about attempts to manipulate the channels of communication, we tend to go along with this. Drawing on Habermas' theory of communicative action, a model describing the normative conditions of engagement for defining and sustaining virtual, networked communities can be developed. This is helpful as it tells us not only what to expect from changing physical communities but also allows us to understand how new digital and social communities form and function within (and beyond) them. Inherent in such a model is the acceptance of models of 'lifeworld' and 'systemworld'; the world of the individual and of the system of society (and government and control) that surrounds it. Where lifeworld is focused on the individual and on communicative action, the systemworld is anonymous, organised and complex, functioning through an instrumentalist form of rationality, yet existing in parallel with the lifeworld, the two operating simultaneously.

Democracy breaks down (some would argue that society breaks down) when the systemworld colonises the lifeworld to the point that individuals are no longer free to communicate, act and interact, where information flows are controlled, restricted and managed and where conversations are contrived, shallow even dangerous. Democracy

---

[8] Habermas, J. (1987). The theory of communicative action: Reason and the rationalization of society). Boston, MA: Beacon.

breaks down when the powerful manage, manipulate and control the conversation and the information needed to engage fully in it. The worst excesses of this are highlighted by Ritzer in his book on the fast-food industry, a business model that is based on conformity, repetition and economy and where the space for individual thought, decision or conversation has been all but eradicated.[9]

In terms of democracy, our actions are at the same time self-contained (in geography and time) and influenced by the complex interactions and power imbalances of the other people involved in them. These are (like us) people who can exist across many communities, both virtual and physical. So, to understand democratic engagement and to reframe it as active democracy, we want to understand the normative dimensions of a community. We want to attempt to understand what occurs within a community. We can think about this in numerous ways but it can include the cognitive mapping of community boundaries and the assumption that we must map multiple boundaries in order to negotiate our world (because we live in multiple communities). The negotiation of these boundaries involves questions such as:

- Who belongs within our community?
- Who belongs to other communities?
- What set of mutual obligations of recognition, respect and trust regulate relations both within and between communities?[10]

The world is complex, multi-dimensional, multi-layered. We take part in different ways in different spaces with different people. The people

---

[9] Ritzer, G. (2000). The McDonaldization of society. Thousand Oaks, CA: Pine Forge Press.
[10] Friedland, L. A. (2001). Communication, community and democracy: Toward a theory of the communicatively integrated community. Communication research, 28(4), 358-301.p.377

we meet and mix with are dispersed. Some, like neighbours or colleagues, we might know primarily face-to-face, others exist solely in a virtual space.

How are we to enter into meaningful debate and dialog with all of these people? How are we to influence and allow ourselves to be influenced deep into and across our networks? How do we connect different and disparate networks? How do we aggregate our ideas to create better collective knowledge? In the next couple of chapters we want to start exploring what active democracy means. We want to discuss power (and why wrong power is a core problem with bad democracy). We're then going to dive right in and talk about the journey that we want to see, the journey that takes democratic systems from arrogant and controlling to intimate and co-creating.

❖ Conversation lies at the heart of active democracies.

❖ It's a complex world and we don't all act and think the same.

❖ Don't get siloed in your thinking, listen carefully and consider what others say. Look at and explore alternative views, recognising that they contain wisdom and energy for realisation.

❖ Authentic dialogue explores differences, leading to understanding and trust.

❖ Do not shy away from the conflicts of interest and trade-offs. Leaders trying to shield and protect us from negative energy, do more harm than good.

❖ If a picture is worth a thousand words, a conversation can be worth a thousand pictures.

What are Active Democracies?

Conversation lies at the heart of democracy. Yes, but democracy as we see it today has been colonised, taken over by powerful vested interests. The result is that it has become a passive experience for many people. High barriers to entry and opaque channels mean that the public are (or feel) largely excluded. Discourse is stifled or manipulated, messages carefully tuned and dispersed by a tame media. To understand how this can change we need to look at how active democracy might work. For us, 'active' means a natural tendency towards co-creation and trust building processes underpinning the way people interact and primarily make decisions. It means a move away from traditional power and hierarchies. These aren't new ideas, in fact it was Aristotle who said, "of mankind in general, the parts are greater than the whole." Aristotle understood the concept of networked democracy.

It's about active 'doing'. What do we mean by this and what do we mean when we say that our current democracies are inactive? Do we mean that people aren't active anymore? Is it fair to say that people aren't engaged in what is happening to them? It clearly wouldn't be right to say that citizens aren't going out to vote in elections (even if this number is falling in most countries and is often particularly low at local and, in the case of Europe, European Parliamentary elections). But the evidence supports a steady drift away from interest in politics and democracy, so what are people doing? It clearly isn't right to say that people aren't active in their communities and there is strong evidence that suggests a sustained rise in 'pressure politics'; those short-sharp actions we take around specific issues.[11] Let's, then, ask two pertinent questions: first, why are people less likely to be engaged with the traditional machinery of democracy? And, second, despite this, how and why are people engaged in other forms of societal or community development?

From our own perspective, people are more engaged than ever! It's just that they're engaged in issues, not ideology. They're engaged in the things that matter to them (and those around them). The channels we now have for demonstration and action are more varied than before. How we show our views and act on our beliefs can now come in a much wider range of flavours. And these different flavours don't fit with the traditional structure of elections, elected officials and compliance or with the decisions made by politicians. They don't fit the formal processes of democracy. The result is that a lot of our legitimate civic action is dismissed by those in power. Which in turn dis-enfranchises people further. What people are doing to make their societies better often happens despite the systems of representative democracy that we have in place. In fact, it is often these systems that are supposed to represent us that we find ourselves fighting against.

Creating momentum around an issue was a slow process 10 years ago, campaigns, demonstrations, petitions, you had to get out in front of the public, wherever they were. It took weeks, months even years. Today all of this can be done digitally through the internet and particularly social media. Facebook and Twitter spread the word, sites like *change.org* help you collect signatures and tools exist that help you mobilise and co-ordinate action. Even text messaging can be a 'killer app' when it comes to mustering supporters at short notice (as we saw in Spain a few years ago with the shock defeat of the incumbent government or in recent protests in the UK against education costs and health service reform).

---

[11] The Power Inquiry. (2006). Power to the people. York: Joseph Rowntree Charitable Trust & Joseph Rowntree Reform Trust.

None of this is really recognised in the formal processes of the 'old' systems. In fact, defenders of the indefensible are quick to dismiss the internet and social media as 'clicktivism', as if stating a view or supporting a cause online is somehow morally, socially – or democratically – inferior to the incumbency. It isn't. The term 'active' has a different meaning now for many of us. Our democratic energy is channelled in new ways, ways in which the current system cannot really comprehend and chooses to downplay even dismiss. This brings to mind two critical words that are vital for a well working society: power and trust. How these two words connect to each other is vital to understanding active democracy.

Power, as we see it expressed, is the glue that bonds society together. Trust is the bridge between differences. With it comes a deepening respect of strongly held views and an acceptance of difference. Power needs to acknowledge alternative views, as being both legitimate and potential perspectives that contain wisdom, energy and solutions. For society to be able to manage itself and cope with issues of social sustainability, the legitimacy of power and the trust between different actors must be addressed and aligned. Active democracy is both a different skill set and a different mind-set for the actors in our society. We've chosen a very strong word to illustrate what we see as the prevailing democratic climate today: arrogance. But arrogance is what we see in the system, its elected officials and civil servants towards the citizens. Arrogance is what happens when power is mis-used and trust dissipates.

In Sweden today (like most Western democracies) there are big and really complex issues that need to be addressed in new ways. And they need to be addressed soon. We can all see the demographic changes: an aging population and fewer people in the tax-generating workforce repeating right across Europe. Yet the basic design of both the welfare and taxation systems is predicated on one generation working and in the process funding social care and welfare for those in the system who cannot work. There is a problem coming and the evidence is that our current systems are struggling to generate solutions that will work. These are complex issues and it is vital for us to see the dimensions of decision-making that surround them. It is important for us to understand the legitimacy of our elected representatives and their officials in the context of societal trust. We see clearly that the level of activity in political parties in Sweden has declined compared to 20 or 30 years ago and the decline appears to be continuing. Today, only one-percent of the Swedish population is an active member of a political party.[12] The UK too has seen a sharp decline in political party membership. After World War II the Conservative Party boasted almost three million members and Labour one million.[13] In 2013 the Conservatives reported as few as 134,000 members. Even in the Prime minister's own constituency membership fell to barely 1,000, leaving the local party with a financial deficit.[14] And this problem isn't unique to Sweden or the UK, it's everywhere. Take a look at how New Zealand's political parties have haemorrhaged members since 1954:[15]

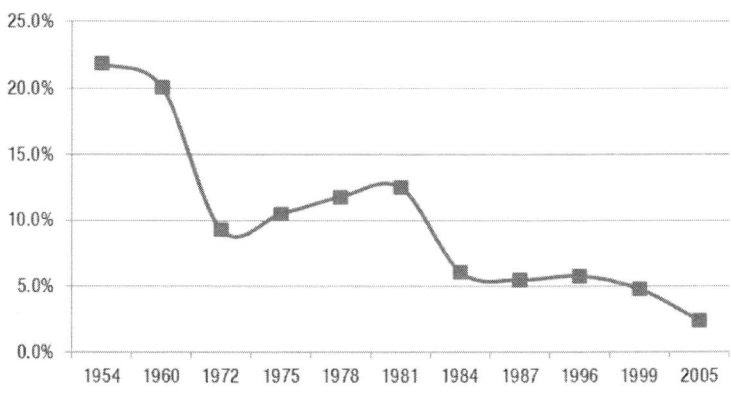

[12] See: Statistiska centralbyråns (www.scb.se).
[13] House of Commons Library. (2012). Membership of UK political parties (SN/5125).
[14] Mason, R. (2014, Jul 12). Members vote with feet and leave party fretting. The Guardian.
[15] Vowles, J. (2002). Parties and society in New Zealand in Political parties in advanced industrial democracies, ed. Webb et al., Oxford: OUP; Miller, R. (2005). Party politics in New Zealand. Oxford: OUP

At the same time as party membership is collapsing, the very legitimacy of decision-making by our elected officials is dependent on their willingness to forego personal power and accept a representative model of power given to them by citizens. Even where voter turnout is relatively high (Sweden and New Zealand have some of the highest levels in the world), the selection of candidates is still restricted to a shrinking elite within political parties.

A key question we are trying to ask ourselves within the work of active democracy is how will the representative democratic system of tomorrow cope with the sustainable challenges our societies are facing? And we are left wanting for an answer. At a recent seminar we were asked if we need a new representative system? As you'll discover here, we're not romantics dreaming about new app-driven digital democracies. We are realists and what we are looking to do is re-energize democracy that actually represents the people, not itself. The real challenges are bringing back the conversations and re-building trust between and in people. There is no "app" for that and neither is abandoning one system for another going to solve the problem either. Is there any legitimacy attached to the people we elect or those who work with them to take the really hard decisions we are going to have to make as societies? For us, it seems that the necessary levels of trust are declining so significantly to the point of this becoming not simply a democratic but a societal crisis.

Power is a critical component of this and we need to understand how it distributed across our society. Power today is present everywhere and nowhere. What do we mean by that? We see power as the ability to do good, to drive through effective change. But all too often it is negative power that we see: the misuse of influence, lobbying and biased messages. Political power is all too often synonymous with bias, personal advantage, even corruption. And power matters because having it gives you influence, and this lets you shape policy – it lets you shape everyone's lives. So when mis-used, as it so often is, power corrupts democracy, turning it into nothing more than a system for achieving personal gains and for perpetuating elites.[16]

Power is not something that you have, power is something that you get. In the Swedish context one percent of people are active in political parties, 99% are not. This raises a serious question of legitimacy. Michel Foucault said of power:

> What makes power hold good, what makes it accepted, is simply the fact it doesn't weigh on us a force that says 'no', but that it traverses and produces things, it induces pleasure, forms knowledge, produces discourse. It needs to be considered as a productive network that runs through the whole social body, much more than as a negative instance whose functions is repression.[17]

Power as a positive energy but today, and especially in politics, power is all too often seen as a zero-sum-game. If I have power, I win. And you lose. What if we leverage Foucault's thinking and consider how we might share power?

What if we think of 'power with' rather than 'power over'? If you share power with others does that mean you lose power? Is power an absolute concept or a relative one? If sharing means losing then we all lose. If we see power as something relative, the more of it that is shared then the stronger it gets – for all of us. Power grows when it is shared, though with this also comes responsibility.

Co-creation and democratic intimacy are not about giving away power, they are about sharing and taking responsibility for how that power is used for good. In this process trust is created through

---

[16] Gilens, M., Page, B.I. (2014). Testing theories of American politics: elites, interest groups, and average citizens. Perspectives on Politics (2014, Fall).
[17] Foucault, M. (1980). Power/knowledge. New York: Pantheon. p.117.

interaction and dialogue. Trust grows naturally as a by-product of authentic action.

Power is not created and it does not operate in a vacuum, it is a process of relationships. It is also an issue of legitimacy because power is often exercised under the authority of the system. Power is not just about information, facts and figures, it's about relationships and our willingness to accept someone else's power over us. Power shared means the power of others is used with us.

Twenty years ago power was retained and contained within the structures of the political parties and amongst a hierarchy. In this system, despite conflicts, actions were largely internally negotiated and citizens accepted the rulings (or did not, in which case an election caused a changed in government). Today power is everywhere and nowhere. It is distributed, diffused, potentially democratised but also manipulated, deflected and spun. Increasingly power is being taken back by citizens and communities who are using new digital and social tools to challenge the hegemonies of power and control in order to usher in a new era of sharing. A new era of collaboration, co-creation and intimacy that sees the old, arrogant and controlling ways of power become unacceptable and untenable.

- ❖ People haven't lost interest in doing, they've lost interest in systems that don't represent them.
- ❖ Active democracy is about getting out there and co-creating better solutions to the stuff we don't like.
- ❖ Active democracies accept and co-create within the conflicts of interest.
- ❖ We don't have to replace representative democracy, we just have to make it more recognisable and more representative from the networked times we live in today.
- ❖ Power used for personal gain will ultimately fail.
- ❖ Power shared is returned with interest and benefits society.

Moving From Arrogance to Intimacy

The traditional models of hierarchical, power-based democracy and governance are dying. The old systems are no longer appropriate, trusted or liked. They are no longer fit for purpose. Whilst society remains stratified, power still lies in the hands of the few and democracy is too often focussed on 'doing to' rather than 'doing with'; more paternalism than partnership (the choice of gender is intentional too). Power, as we have discussed, is a problem, a negative drain on the good name of democracy and, ironically, democratic drift gives those with the power even more of it. But distributed power, used well, lies at the heart of the opportunity.

This outdated world is one of arrogance and control. Decisions are made by a small group of people, either elected, appointed or anointed. Information is gathered from a small range of safe sources and trusted intermediaries. Debate is not widely encouraged. This is a system rife with bias and imbalance. Lending itself to political favour and ideological hi-jacking. At its worst the arrogance of incumbency and the pursuit of power leads to corruption, nepotism and poor decision making. Even at its supposed best it's ideological and intellectual elitism, arrogance and a valuing of technocracy over democracy and the citizens it is supposed to serve.

Democracy comes with high barriers to entry and is too often focussed on power plays and a deficit-based discourse. No wonder it's a turn-off to an excluded public.

How can this change? How can we create democratic systems that are intimate, not arrogant, that are open, accessible and co-creational, not closed and controlling? How do we make our democracy interactive, co-creative and powered by positive power? The answer isn't simple and at its heart there is a burning need for cultural transformation. But that doesn't mean the building blocks to a new way of democracy have to be complex.

Let's start this journey by moving our democratic system from one firmly stuck in control to one that values a wider contribution from more people, one that lends itself to co-creativity. This journey has already started in a few places, in small ways, accelerated by the advent of new digital and social media that bring people closer to the conversation, make sharing easier and distribute knowledge in ways that were unimaginable a generation ago. It's supported by new ways of thinking about power relations and by an increased yearning for a new way of operating. Whilst technology is a vital enabler it's the latter human, social, power-based shifts that will both accelerate, disrupt and embed real transformation.

New digital and social spaces have supported some movement where limited listening widens the net of those who can be involved. Limited flexibility sees democratic institutions reach out beyond their traditional methods of engagement, bringing others into the debate earlier. But both of these models are built around an agenda where governments remain in control and still direct the nature and determine the scale of engagement. They are a first step on the path, they are not the journey.

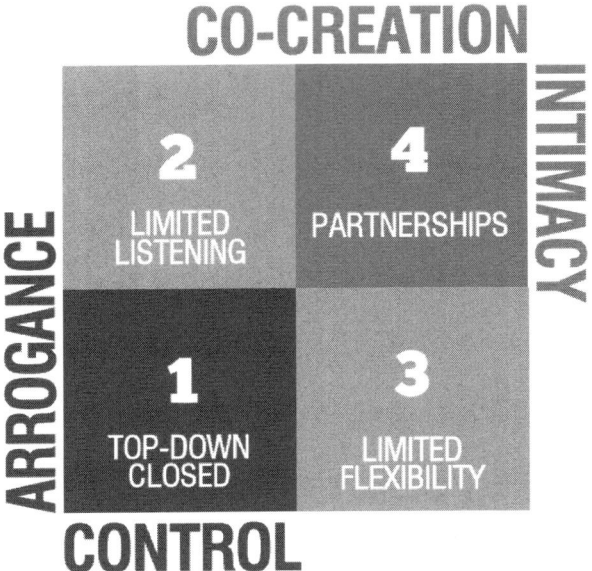

In active democracies, engagement and therefore governance is a grounded partnership. Government is an equal partner. Equal with citizens. Government is one piece in the democratic jigsaw. An important part, yes, but no longer in charge. Suddenly an opportunity emerges to become the facilitator of change in a newly forming landscape.

Take Denmark's MindLab as an example, it was established as a cross-departmental innovation unit by the Danish government and is now a partnership between three Ministries and the Odense Municipality. It focuses on creating new solutions for government by involving citizens and businesses. MindLab helps to give a fresh perspective to public service delivery and has created a model that allows those on the inside to see the world from the perspective of those on the outside.[18]

---

[18] See: www.mind-lab.dk

This new landscape is not without its challenges. Trust is crucial, yet it has fallen to all-time low levels. If it worries you that only a quarter of people in the UK trust their politicians, it should concern you even more that in a new democracy, Serbia, it's only 8%.

Much of the friction in civil society comes from inadequate engagement processes. People feel dis-empowered, they feel disconnected. They have been cut adrift. Changing this requires more than a new tool, a fancy smartphone 'app' or mechanism, change requires a demonstrable commitment over time.

We have to start small and build up. Change comes incrementally and there is no single solution, no switch that can be turned on to re-charge democracy. The failure, disconnect and decay go too deep.

So why become intimate? Why does it matter? We're not suggesting that everything that government does has to be 100% participatory and co-created. That would be crazy! Sometimes people just have to make decisions and get on with it. That is in fact why we elect them, pay leaders more. Even when we distrust politicians research shows us that citizens are often happy to leave them too it a lot of the time.

It's about balance. There are times when we need to do stuff together, do stuff with more people, listen to more people, talk to more people and look at the widest range of data, the broadest range of stories that we can get our hands on. Because doing this achieves a number of things:

- More information, managed properly leads to better decisions
- More interactive policy making means more appropriate service delivery
- Better service design reduces costs

And then there's one less obvious but no less important benefit:

- Involving people in deciding what their world looks like gives them a sense of ownership over the outcome.

And all of this starts to build trust.

Moving from arrogance to intimacy – from control to co-creation – is not a binary shift. It's movement along a continuum. The further along that continuum we are able to work comfortably, then the more options we have available. Old-world, closed, controlling government – arrogant government – has little room for manoeuvre, limited sources of information and limited skills and knowledge available to understand, design and implement new policies and services.

Compare this to the co-designed organisation, no longer constricted by silos, limited thinking and fear. Active democracies are networked democracies, now we can put the question out to many people in multiple formats, we can get others to ask the questions (their own not just ours) and they can in turn bring back to the conversation (because conversation lies at the heart of active democracy).

New ideas, new data, new stories, new people. Ideas, data, stories and people who were previously off our radar and out of reach. Yes, this requires a new attitude and new models for engagement but remember no one person, group or organisation owns the process anymore, there are plenty of people out there who can help us design it, build it and make it happen, if we let them in!

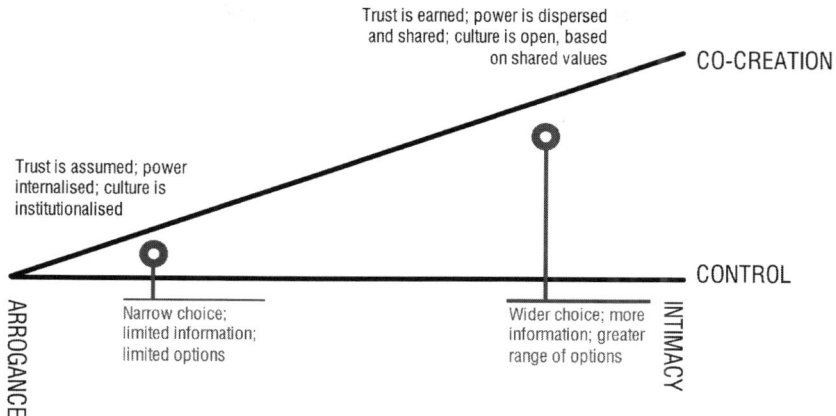

Trust is earned; power is dispersed and shared; culture is open, based on shared values — CO-CREATION

Trust is assumed; power internalised; culture is institutionalised

CONTROL

ARROGANCE

Narrow choice; limited information; limited options

Wider choice; more information; greater range of options

INTIMACY

In the old world, trust is assumed, power is internalised, held on to. There is an institutional culture of power, politics and hierarchy. But trust has been lost, politics is seen as divisive and power corrupts. In the new system trust is earned through mutuality, co-creation and by demonstrable action. Power is dispersed around those in the process based on contribution, skills and knowledge. The culture is based on co-operation and shared values, it looks for a vision not necessarily consensus. It looks to harness the whole community in making decisions real. To do this it values the skills, knowledge and experiences of all the community.

There are a number of stages to democratic transformation, the roles people take on and how these change and evolve as the process shifts and matures (we'll talk about this a lot more in the chapter on 'Why Personal Engagement Matters'). We liken it to an addiction model, where you have to recognise there's a problem before you can seek to change and relapse is always a risk! When we map this across our continuum from arrogance to intimacy, we start to see the roles and actions that support an active democracy culture. What we need to be in order to be intimate, co-creating and interactive, so power can be shared for positive change.

	STATUS QUO	BUILD UP	ACTION	MAINTENANCE
GOVERNMENT	ARROGANT	RESISTANT	ENGAGING	INTIMATE
CITIZEN	DIS-ENGAGED	CHALLENGING	ENGAGING	CO-CREATING
REBEL/ INNOVATOR	CHALLENGING	DISRUPTING	QUESTIONING	
REFORMER		AWARENESS BUILDING	TRANSFORMING PROCESS	
CHANGE AGENT		CONNECTING	LEADING DIALOGUE	SUPPORTING

We can see that the arrogant government/dis-engaged citizen dialectic – the place where we're starting from – needs waking up to change. In the civic sense, we've described the role of the 'rebel' who leads the protest, raises the issues and campaigns loudly for wider recognition of perceived problem or injustice. What we see now is that public institutions need their own rebels too, people who can challenge the status quo, develop new and radical approaches to democratic engagement, service design and delivery. These people are the intrapreneurs and innovators. And like society's rebels, they often face a steep climb to gain recognition. A key part of active democracies is building systems that hold these people and their ideas close and feed innovation from all sides into the system. A networked democracy is a system that embraces and encourages innovation.

We're convinced that what must happen here is diffusion, dissemination and, above all, conversation. Active democracies rely on an innovation eco-system, open to all and based on collaboration, co-operation and social benefit. To make democracy fit for today, we've got to put these at the heart of what we do.

In the next section of this book we want to discuss the disconnection of citizens to politics and democracy. The issues and challenges that we face and must overcome if the ideals discussed above are to have a hope of setting in place a new, more open, co-creative and intimate democracy.

- ❖ Democracy has been arrogant and controlling for too long.
- ❖ We need systems that are intimate and co-creating if people are to reconnect.
- ❖ Democratic systems will be better and more responsive and creative if more people are connected to them.
- ❖ We need new attitudes, new models continuous innovation from all sides.
- ❖ From stronger connections comes greater trust and ability to thrive from diversity.
- ❖ Networks are stronger and more resilient than silos. Interconnected worlds, work through networks.

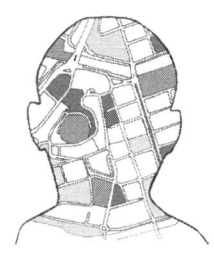

How We Became
Disconnected

A Problem of Language

Since the 1980s many of our 'developed' democracies have shifted radically away from a prevailing culture of community towards a culture of individualism. We are living in the most connected times ever seen and yet, in some ways, we seem to be more disconnected from each other than ever. The extent of connection and disconnection, trust and disillusionment varies across the world but our own experience tells us the patterns are remarkably similar across the UK, Sweden, Australia and Aotearoa New Zealand, they just manifest in different ways and at different times. From falling voter turnout to the rise of alternative extremist political parties and the outbreak of rioting in London, Stockholm and Gothenburg, how social unrest is rising in Australia and constant tension between Maori and non-Maori remains a potent disrupting force in a rapidly expanding multi-cultural Aotearoa New Zealand.

The World Values Survey tells us that Sweden is unique in its extreme values of self-actualization and secular rationalism.[19] In the UK, the social failures of neo-liberalism could draw their epitaph from Margaret Thatcher's infamous quote, "there is no such thing as society".[20] Today this jars so much with our sense of civic value that even some inheritors of her British Conservative torch feel obliged to distance themselves from it.

---

[19] See: www.worldvaluessurvey.org
[20] Interview with Woman's Own, September 1987 (transcript available at: margaretthatcher.org/document/106689)

But the fact remains that we are no longer *just* citizens. We are today framed as consumers of government and democracy. And this is a problem. The rationalisation of public services into efficient 'business units' has paralleled a rise in the role of a technocratic elite. And this has come at the expense of participation and trust.

It has led to a subtle but insidious shift in our language, referring to us as 'customers' and government as a 'business' that delivers a 'service'. This kind of language isn't just about the wholesale transformation of government, once established in the everyday lexicon, outsourced, corporatized and commercial 'government' enterprise suddenly seems less unpalatable. We are privatising the public sector through language.

But government isn't a 'business' and we are not simply 'customers'. The difference is democracy. Genuine examples do exist of good attempts to engage the public but these are the outliers and they are too few. Is it any wonder that citizens often feel that their governments are arrogant, controlling, distant?

Even within the democratic context we have to be careful with language. 'Consultation' means different things to different people and terms such as 'deliberative democracy' carry a wealth of baggage. Even the word 'democracy' is a contestable discourse, it's definition transient, personal and open to capture, mis-use and manipulation.

Governments aren't innocent parties here, they often distrust the public and prefer the expertise of select groups of (often ex-government) consultants, NGOs and experts. Even when the public are consulted this is narrowly scoped, restricted in terms of time and space and the primacy of expert opinion de-values citizens' views. All re-enforcing those feelings of dislocation and dis-engagement.

- We're citizens, not customers.
- Democracy is not a business model.
- Focusing on the technical aspects of democracy causes people to feel alienated.
- Trust has failed on both sides.
- Language holds and conveys power and control.

Civic Disconnection

As we've said, our democratic paradox is that the most connected society in history often feels more splintered and disconnected than ever. A strong civil society is a sign of a healthy democracy but the pressures on a changing public landscape have reduced opportunities for citizens to be engaged, debate and modify their beliefs as a group – as a community. Consultation is now often done through NGOs, academics and lobbyists.

Does this matter? Isn't it acceptable to consult via interest groups and those with expert knowledge and to rely on this expertise to make the best decisions for our communities? Yes, to a degree. But how are we to ensure that they represent all the views, not just those of a privileged few, not just the loudest voices. And who is to decide what we mean by 'expert'?

It matters too because an active civil society gives us:

1. better and more responsive services;
2. less disengagement from the democratic process; and
3. stronger social capital.[21]

All good things.

---

[21] Skidmore, P., Bound, K., & Lownsbrough, H. (2006) Community participation: Who benefits? Joseph Rowntree Foundation: York, UK.

But surely the NGOs and interest groups are part of civil society, aren't they? Well, yes and no! Many civil society organisations have bought into the technocratic arguments of government. They position themselves as the 'experts' of choice when it comes to representing the views of a wider public. All of this happens regardless of the extent to which we've actually been consulted or consented to be represented (and it often suits the government not to ask too many questions on that front).

This shift towards the professionalization of civil society has been a direct response to neoliberalism and its resultant "socio-spatial polarisation".[22] And it's a double-edged sword. In addition to the rise of activist organisations, neoliberalism has led to a significant increase in neo-communitarian service-based NGOs, focusing on social cohesion and framed within a civil society context that, whilst strengthened, is reliant on strategic compacts (neo-Faustian contracts, perhaps?) with local and national government. These organisations might work for the good of our communities but they are effectively blackmailed into silence, unable to criticise government for risk of losing their funding.

The big NGOs are corporatized, run by professional managers, and able to orchestrate significant campaigns to effect influence and affect government policy in their areas of interest. So membership of these campaign organisations serves two purposes; first, it suggests a level of support and, therefore, importance and power and, second, it brings in revenue to allow campaigns to be funded. But there is no inherent pre-requisite for NGOs to act democratically themselves; most supporters give money but take no active role or oversight in the organisation.

Social capital is often embodied in the key relationships that exist between individuals or organisations across civil society, access to it is,

---

[22] Larner, W. & Craig, D. (2005) After neoliberalism? Community activism and local partnerships on Aotearoa New Zealand. Antipode, 37(3): p. 402-423.

therefore, negotiated via a range of background factors that include socio-economic status, geographical circumstances, ethnicity, religion, age, gender and sexual orientation. If democratic conversations are open only to an inside elite, no matter who that elite is, then we have a problem. Power across the democratic system is not evenly distributed.

Of course, we're not suggesting that NGOs are bad. Or that they aren't a vital component of the democratic landscape. We're simply saying that caution is needed when such organisations claim to 'represent' citizens.

We're highlighting too that there has been a steady polarisation between 'grassroots' civil society and corporatized NGOs. This is seen best in movements such as 38 Degrees[23], which is not only member-driven but has turned the UK campaigning sector upside down. Through its innovative use of networked social media and good old-fashioned emails directly into the inboxes of the decision makers and legislators it has managed to create engagement and to build awareness in ways that the established monoliths of the NGO sector have, frankly, failed to do.

Another example is 'House Party 14', a UK collective of social activists. Organised as an unofficial fringe conference, this ran alongside the Chartered Institute of Housing's annual housing conference. Their aim was to bring together "the widest possible collaborators of grassroots housing and social change-makers to explore and solve some of the most pressing needs in UK housing".[24] The sub-text is clear: the official conference was not inclusive, not giving a fair voice to everyone and was perpetuating the status quo at a time when many felt a radical new approach was needed.

---

[23] See: 38degrees.org.uk
[24] See: houseparty2014.org

Neither of these examples are part of the system and they inevitably create friction and meet resistance. But some resistance is a good thing, particular when the system is dysfunctional and failing. The challenge is recognising the point at which it becomes counter-productive. In other words, you have managed to engage and a different approach is needed.

An ideal civil society, a resilient and strong civil society, reflects an inter-connection of individuals and groups, with varying degrees of formality and structure. There is room in this model for the established NGOs but there is also an inherent shift away from monolithic structures so that new, viral, explosive social movements can come and go, can challenge assumptions and values and contest "the modality of the social use of resources and cultural models".[25] Or, as Billy Bragg put it, "start your own revolution, cut out the middleman".[26]

If legislators don't have all the answers, and NGOs don't really represent us, then there is role for individual citizens, informal groups of citizens and independent campaign organisations to step in, step up and raise the profile of issues amongst a wider, sceptical public. But to be effective they must have ways to engage with the formal processes of government; simply being a permanent protestor or rebel achieves little. Real change requires partnership and shared understanding.

[25] Touraine, A. (2000) Can we live together? Equality and difference. Oxford: Polity. p.90.
[26] Billy Bragg, Waiting for the great leap forward. Workers playtime (1988).

- ❖ A strong civil society is a sign of a healthy democracy.
- ❖ We need to question who really represents us and challenge those who don't but claim to.
- ❖ We have to broaden the input to policy development and decision making.
- ❖ New issues-based collectives using social media are creating new ways to challenge and engage.

Psst... Want Some Evidence?

Governments like evidence. Good, solid, strong, scientific evidence. Numbers are good. Lots of numbers, analyses of these numbers with expert interpretations attached, obviously. But our focus on 'evidence-based' policy is not without danger. Constantly looking for data to identify 'best practice' can cause us to lose sight of 'next practices', pushing us towards mimicry and mediocrity. Innovation comes from having the heart and courage to do something differently. No amount of sophistication is going to allay the dichotomy between all your knowledge being based on the past and all your decisions being about the future. Today's democracies seem to us to be over-investing in 'business as usual', in maintaining the status quo, rather than exploring alternative views and different ways of doing. And this makes them controlling and arrogant, in their values and actions.

If this is the case, who decides what is and isn't acceptable evidence? What does 'scientific' actually mean and is it the right measure anyway? How do we know that our public servants have done the full sweep of available evidence, citing with equal weight the pros and the cons? How do we ensure that politicians are not 'front loading' the policy system for their own political ends?

How do we ensure that so-called 'think-tanks' are open about their agenda and where their funding comes from?[27] Are they honest about

---

[27] We'll talk about think tanks specifically in the next chapter.

their aims and not just out to produce biased, pre-determined results in order to promote a narrow ideological position?

How can we avoid colonisation of decision making by positivists overly embedded in the 'scientific method' at the exclusion of all else? How do we assess the credibility of all this research? You only have to look at the medical research industry (and it really is an industry!) to know that even so-called rigorous academic research all too often lacks credibility and objectivity by the time it's selectively published.

Above all, how do we avoid the trap of policy-based evidence? Just consider the UK's Department for the Environment, Food and Rural Affairs (DEFRA). DEFRA has been engaged in a cull of badgers to prevent tuberculosis (TB) in cattle which is, we are told, evidence based. Yet there appears to be an almost complete lack of accepted scientific evidence to support the efficacy of such a policy. In fact there is overwhelming scientific evidence against it. There is even evidence to suggest that a partial cull makes the TB situation in cattle worse. There is also overwhelming public disagreement with the policy. Unfortunately, it just happens that the poor old badgers living in the 'pilot' cull areas have wealthy, land-owning farmers for neighbours. These people vote, badgers don't. Coincidence? You decide. Credible evidence-based policy, or simply policy-based evidence? Again, you decide![28]

Let's take another example, again from the UK Government, only this time the Department for Work and Pensions (DWP). Criticised in 2013 by Parliament "for a series of rule breaches in which official statistics were used inaccurately, inappropriately, or to 'spin' stories about

---

[28] Monbiot, G. (2013, Sep 30). For scientists in a democracy, to dissent is to be reasonable. The Guardian: www.theguardian.com/commentisfree/2013/sep/30/scientists-democracy-dissent-reasonable-boyd

benefit claimants."[29] The UK Statistics Authority, whose statutory role includes vetting the accuracy of government statistics has been highly critical of DWP in its assessments on a number of occasions.[30]

So what does constitute valid evidence? We need a broad definition because an emphasis on 'scientific' evidence and 'research' cements the position of the technocrats in government. And it does so at the expense of people. We're not arguing that rigorous academic and scientific evidence isn't valid. It clearly is. But it's important to see this as just one input to the process and to treat it as such. We've got to avoid reifying one type of evidence or data over others, because it only ever tells one part of the story.

How then are we to give weight and value to social and embedded research – to people – and to the folksonomies, stories and narratives of our communities as well? After all, policy is about real life and people's lives (despite what some people think) cannot be properly understood through multivariate analysis alone.

How do we generate new understanding, new knowledge and feed co-created ideas into our governance systems rather than repeating the mistakes of the past?

The insular reliance on narrow sources of policy advice matters. Only a minority of UK citizens want to be involved in decision making. Alongside wide-spread distrust, dis-engagement and plummeting political party membership (the Conservatives have gone from three million to 200,000 in twenty years!), political campaigning has been transformed into brand management and marketing. This sees the

---

[29] Butler, P. (2013, Mar 18). MPs criticise DWP for 'spin' on official statistics and benefit claimant. The Guardian: theguardian.com/politics/2014/mar/18/mps-criticise-dwp-spin-statistics-benefit-claimants

[30] BBC News. (2014, Jul 3). Small Data: DWP leads the way on statistical complaints. www.bbc.co.uk/news/blogs-magazine-monitor-28061826

voter as a consumer and policy is too often mediated through media commentary that more closely resembles sports punditry than it does serious debate. Political communication throughout the now perpetual electoral cycle has a focus on re-election and blame.[31]

Democratic disaffection is not "a story of the decline of civic virtue, nor is it a story of political apathy – it is one of disenchantment, even hatred, of politics and politicians".[32]

As we said earlier, numbers are often a good way to make a point, so let's look at some that paint a stark picture of our attitude to democracy: In the UK, 73% of citizens are dis-satisfied with the democratic system. Although 63% agree that they have a duty to get involved when democracy isn't working and 60% believe that we must get involved for the system to improve, only 29% of us believe that giving citizens more of a say will have any positive impact. This is hardly surprising when 85% of UK citizens feel that they exert little or no influence over government decisions and more than half of Britons (55%) believe that politics and government is too hard to understand.[33]

Not all information is created equal.

[31] Gaber, I. (2007). Too much of a good thing: The 'problem' of political communications in a mass media democracy. Journal of Public Affairs, 2007(7): p. 219-234.
[32] Hay, C, Stoker, G, & Williamson, A. (2008). Revitalising politics: Have we lost the plot? Paper presented at Revitalising Politics conference, London
[33] Hansard Society. (2013). Audit of Political Engagement. Hansard Society: London

- ❖ Who defines the value of different types of 'data'?
- ❖ Scientific data is good but that does not make human experience bad.
- ❖ Policy must reflect the lived and social experience as well as the analysis.
- ❖ The public dislikes that politics has become a culture of blame.
- ❖ Beware of policy-based evidence.

The Problem with Think-Tanks

Think tanks have become a familiar site in the space between citizens and government. But they are not neutral: who is funding them, what is their agenda and how good is their research? Three critical questions we must ask of every organisation that seeks to influence the democratic agenda.

Think tanks do, however, provide a significant and valuable contribution in the policy space. Operating well, they are both creators of new knowledge and a conduit for smart thinking on future direction so it's worth taking some time to think about think tanks and how one might function in a world of active democracies.

To differentiate yourself in the market (and, yes, it is a market) many of the political think tanks stake out ideological positions. That's great so long as the ideology is in favour but when the tide turns you're forced to turn with it and run for higher ground. This is exactly what has happened to those on the left in the UK over the last few years. As a result, the political centre is now rather crowded. But just to show that lessons aren't being learned, we've seen a profusion of right-of-centre think tanks rise to prominence. Well guess where they're heading! Don't know when, but they're heading there.

Of course, a strong ideological position is a perfectly reasonable thing. It can be a smart move in the short and even medium term. It gives you a platform and a platform makes you attractive to certain groups, individuals or organisations. And they might fund you. Or give your ideas publicity, which helps you get funding. The alternative is to remain neutral and non-partisan. A valid approach but being neutral can make you less attractive to interest groups. Less hostage to fortune, it means that you can focus more on the processes at work behind the scenes and be less swayed by popular (or populist) agendas. There's potential here to create real change in the long term. And of course, the aim of a think tank is for someone to do something based on something you thought. Isn't it?

There's a second problem with the non-partisan model. Being less 'sexy', less 'outspoken' (generally non-partisan means non-radical too) means that you are more attractive to institutional funders, such as government departments. That's good isn't it? Well, no, because it's fickle (and it risks throwing think tanks in to the same neo-Faustian pacts as NGOs that we discussed earlier). Right now they're not funding nearly as much nearly as often (if at all). But the biggest flaw is that it ties a hand behind your back, requiring a difficult course to be plotted between a sufficiently vocal critique to be worth bothering with and not gnawing too hard on the paymaster's sensitive hand.

The next problem with think tanks is that they can appear out of touch. They are, after all, dealing with ideas – theory – not actually 'doing' anything. This is a fair criticism but the problem is more nuanced. If the think tank in question is grounded enough and maintains good connections with those that actually do the things they are theorising about then its fine, praxis based is perhaps the most valuable model. All too often though they maintain good relations with only one side of the equation. This is caused in large part by the fourth problem; elitism.

Think tanks don't employ a representative sample of the population. You've got to be interested in politics (or government, or whatever), university educated etc. But even saying that, the playing field is positively alpine and the problem starts right up front.

Think tanks are inveterate users of interns, often unpaid. And whilst, done properly, the opportunity this presents is invaluable it's possibly the most exclusionary and elitist system short of British Public Schools. Which is where too many of these interns come from, because without good financial backing (read: wealthy parents), it's virtually impossible to do a three or four month unpaid internship in London or Washington. And it's getting harder. The whole system perpetuates an odious and unacceptable elitism in the Westminster (or Brussels, Washington or Canberra) bubble that is as much a part of the democratic problems we have as candidate selection and wider voter disaffection.

Then we come to the problem of thinking versus doing. Think tanks need to be critical, imaginative, creative places where a culture of new ideas is backed up by rigorous research and insight is developed. Creating this kind of buzz is what makes a think tank space special, lose it and you become tired, boring and ineffectual. Dilute it too much with operational matters and you lose the spark. Managing the different cultures of thinking and doing can be highly problematic. Many think tanks avoid this dilemma by doing nothing. That's a reasonable response so long as someone is using your work. Attempting to create revenue streams that operationalise projects and programmes out of research, whilst a good idea, causes tension and needs careful management. To effectively instantiate the intellectual capital they generate think tanks need clear pathways into 'do tanks' that ensure that rigour and intellectual stamina are not diluted. These are more often than not missing and think tanks become reliant on others to instantiate their ideas and act upon them.

We've focussed on the problems that we believe prevent think-tanks being as effective as they could be. That often prevents them being useful (in the big picture sense). So, let's put some balance into the debate and put forward some thoughts on what an alternative model might look like.

The biggest challenge is always going to be monetising critical thought. And this remains a problem regardless of the model, so rather than wasting acres of real estate trying to solve this one right now let's just state the obvious: it's a balancing act of income over expenditure. As Charles Dickens said, you get these wrong and you're in trouble. Translating this into the real world and we would rather be impressed by the intellectual capacity of the product than the offices the think-tank lives in. There's more than one London or Washington think tank that would do well to dwell on this for a moment.

The other big expense is staff, hence the drive towards junior and low or no-cost interns. But this affects quality. So the answer here should be somewhat self-explanatory, which is to start moving towards virtual think tank models drawing in the best to solve the problem at hand. Obviously that's a simplistic statement and needs more thought, but it can be done – this model works in other disciplines (we know, we've done it).

We can draw on ideas of social networks, crowd sourcing and gaming theory to manage the people, processes and to produce intellectually rigorous work in a cost effective way. There are well developed models of open publishing that will allow not just finished work but also the underlying thought processes and data to be published so that they are transparent and accessible to anyone. Transparency can go beyond data to include analysis too.

Surprisingly (or perhaps not) balance is often a missing component. This can be achieved through the virtual, socially networked model we're suggesting above. It is possible to bring together different and competing ideological positions to tackle the same problems. There are ways to manage this process virtually that can assure the outcome is rigorous and free of overall bias or narrowed thought. A key part of ensuring the veracity and credibility of the work is to be able to unpack any assertions, drill down through what has been written to understand on what the assertion is based – opinion, meta-data, fact.

Surely anyone wanting to really understand all sides of a policy issue would value a product like that and with lower overheads it would also be a more commercially viable proposition too?

- ❖ Opaque funding structures and hidden agendas render think-tanks unfit for purpose.
- ❖ Policy development must be as rigorous and transparent outside government as it is inside the civil service.
- ❖ Independent thinking is vital but legitimately monetising a think tank is difficult.
- ❖ There are potential new models for think tanks to use crowd-sourcing and exist virtually.

A Brief Warning about Digital Panaceas

Yes, digital is good; it matters. It changes lots. But it's not a panacea and, on its own at least, it's not a solution. Despite its innovative label much digital democracy has turned out to be little more than a glossy coat of paint, hastily applied to the rusting hulk of democracy. New tools, websites and apps are lauded as effective ways of overcoming the democratic deficit, capable of engaging the public more closely in political processes. In reality they often end up as little more than placebos bolted on to systems and processes that are out of date, out of touch and failing.

This is because what's wrong with democracy can't be fixed with a new 'app'.

The raison d'être for digital democracy is better democracy. Not more digital. So unless digital solutions are part of a holistic and transformative process that ensures democratic systems are accessible, accountable, open and transparent then they can only ever have a limited impact.

We've got to see the system not the transaction, change the culture not the website.

There are some significant examples of how activists using new technology have improved the democratic process and brought conversations about openness and transparency to the table. Whilst it might seem passé today, when MySociety created 'FixMyStreet' it marked a radical and significant departure in the relationship between local government and citizens. For the first time it gave a sizable portion of the general public not just direct access to their local government but direct control over what civil servants were hearing. The same was true for 'TheyWorkForYou', it gave an interested public far easier access to the proceedings of Parliament and an understanding of how their representatives voted. This and other examples are today spawning significant developments in Parliamentary monitoring, not just in developed countries where we take democracy for granted but (and perhaps most excitingly) in developing democracies. This matters because the nascent nature of the political process in these countries means that nothing is certain and the risks of corruption, manipulation and, indeed, democratic failure remain high.

One of our biggest failures has been to continually bolt another technical solution over the top of our democratic problems. This leads to failure because technological determinism doesn't work. Creating interesting technological solutions simply because you can isn't enough. It isn't any good. Technology only becomes normative when it works for a significant percentage of the people affected by a problem that it can elegantly solve, mitigate or side-step. Texting is perhaps the classic example of this. We've got to recognise the social value, the social benefit, not the technical elegance (which isn't to say that usability doesn't matter, gov.uk shows us that it does). Many were critical of gov.uk winning a design award? Is it really that radical? Well, yes, perhaps it is, because the focus has been on building a solution from the ground up where what the citizen needs is the focus, not the technology or the civil servant.

None of this is a criticism of technologists: we need them. But as part of a bigger team. We need more people who passionately believe that democracy can be improved through the use of new digital tools. Their motives are genuine and their ambitions positive. But to do things better we need more. We need those who understand the strategic picture, the policy and the human perspective to partner with the technologists and support them to always think beyond the digital. If you get the 'why' then help those who can deliver the 'what' and 'how'.

We believe that digital is such a significant disrupter of the status quo and an enabler of innovation and change. It's not a panacea and technology, to work, has to align, enhance and support the underlying social and democratic process but it opens up opportunities today that simply did not exist yesterday. That's why we want to focus on the role of digital in creating and realising active democracies in the next section.

❖ What's wrong with democracy can't be fixed with a new app!

❖ It's not about digital, it's about culture.

❖ We have to design with the user in mind from the start.

❖ It's about collaboration, technologist, designers, policy makers and citizens doing stuff together.

❖ Make it all open and build your technology so others can build upon it.

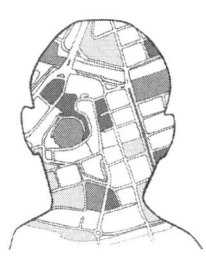

Enabling Networked Democracy

Situating Online Engagement

Use of the internet has become normative; it is impossible to imagine major events happening today without it having a role. We might not, in Europe at least, have 'digital elections', despite the picture that the media tries to paint, but we very much do have elections that are shaped by digital tools and which would look quite different without them.[34] The internet is not of itself responsible for social change but the level of change and of speed we're experiencing simply could not happen without it. The internet speeds up social change as a super-connector, showing us that we are not alone. However, this merely reflects changes in society; we are not driven by technology rather by the social appropriation of various technologies based on perceived value (individually and collectively).

The internet has evolved into a social space but to make it an effective democratic space – a platform for citizen engagement – it must also become a set of channels and tools for collaboration. This means going beyond the networked and the social to ensure open access to information – particularly data sets – so that core groups of connected individuals can repackage and make these available for others to use. There are issues of locus and scale involved; for many individuals engagement first happens on a very local level but social media allows this to grow and for active citizens to be better connected with like minds, supported from afar to use the tools effectively.

---

[34] Gibson, R. K., Williamson, A., & Ward, S. (Eds.). (2010). The internet and the 2010 election: Putting the small 'p' back in politics? London: Hansard Society.

Some fear that the internet is leading to a fragmentation of the public sphere, others simply point out that it enables a more organic form of political engagement. One that fosters engagement by and for local communities. Rather than assume that diverse groups and opinions require shepherding into a unitary public sphere (and we've already said, there isn't a single public sphere anyway), advocates of internet-enabled governance suggest that areas of civic interest can congregate online and that networks will emerge that lead to new forms of engagement.

There is some truth in this logic but we have to be careful not to become technologically deterministic in our approach. No technology, no matter how good, creates change, people do. And the internet does not of itself change an individual's motivation to become engaged, what it does is reduce the barriers to engagement and hence lower the motivational threshold at which citizens choose to engage.[35] Such re-invigoration of civil society can itself be a catalyst for democratic renewal and, as Sunstein argues, the internet in this regard is at least not bad for democracy.[36]

As far back as 2002 the British Government suggested that new media could support a restructuring of the relationship between citizens and state:

> [An] e-Democracy policy should be viewed in a context of those political and constitutional reforms, which seek to devolve power, extend citizens' rights and improve the transparency and accountability of government and politics.[37]

---

[35] Williamson, A. (2007). Empowering communities to action: Reclaiming local democracy through ICTs, in Community Informatics Research Conference. Prato, Italy.
[36] Sunstein, C.R. (2001). Republic.com. Princeton, NJ: Princeton University Press.
[37] Cabinet Office. (2002). In the service of democracy. London: TSO

The Hansard Society's Digital Dialogues project – a three-year study of online government engagement – highlighted the benefits of what happens when citizens and government *do* talk online.[38] If makes it clear that this can be beneficial to both sides and shows why there is a need for a more sustained public deliberation with government. Standing in the way of this 'effective engagement' are barriers on both sides. On the government side, these include a lack of 'buy in' to the principles of true engagement and a culture that is inherently averse to risk – and which perceives engaging with a non-expert public as high risk.

The internet too facilitates the kinds of single-issue politics that are becoming increasingly popular offline and which do not necessarily link back to traditional democratic processes or institutions. Instead, citizen-led online activism tends to be viral and anarchic, leading to a distributed model of political individualism.[39] Nor do new technologies necessarily lead to an increase in the numbers of people participating. The internet provides access to far more information but the overload arising from this could account for a reduction in participation.[40] Information is often conflicting and contradictory, yet it appears to be online human-nature to congregate around like-minds, rather than to actively seek out difference.[41]

[38] Miller, L., & Williamson, A. (2008). Digital Dialogues Third Phase Report. London: Hansard Society & Ministry of Justice

[39] Williamson, A. (2011). Disruption and empowerment: Embedding citizens at the heart of democracy. Journal of eDemocracy and Open Government.

[40] Bimber, B. (1998). The Internet and political transformation: Populism, community and accelerated pluralism. Polity, XXXI(1), 133-160.

[41] Witschge, T. (2002, 9-12 October). Online deliberation: Possibilities of the Internet for deliberative democracy. Paper presented at the Euricom Colloquium: Electronic Networks and Democratic Engagement, Nijmegen, Netherlands.

- ❖ The social nature of the internet makes it an ideal place to engage people.
- ❖ Networks lie at the heart of active democracies and the internet is a powerful tool for creating and sustaining networks.
- ❖ The internet makes single-issue campaigns much easier to start and scale.
- ❖ When governments engage authentically, citizens appreciate it and engage themselves.
- ❖ Beware of information overload and recognise the importance of information literacy.

The Benefits of Digital Engagement

The clearest benefits of digital engagement are better policy outcomes and better service design and delivery, through to more engaged and empowered citizens. Research shows many clear benefits to digital engagement when it is well planned and executed. Digital communication deepens engagement with those who are already interested in the issues being addressed and it offers the potential to reach new audiences who might otherwise not contribute.

Digital and social media allows both government agencies and civil society to break the stranglehold of the mainstream media. Indeed, the media is increasingly seen to be following and responding to issues that become visible first on social networks. There is a practical value to this for engagement in that it means strategies can be more targeted and direct and that the delivery cost is lowered. Using digital media effectively gives you greater control over the information and communication agenda.

Digital media provide significant opportunities not just to distribute information and to seek responses but also to listen. Listening to social media and informal channels, such as Twitter streams and blogs, allows engagement and communication strategies to be more effectively targeted and provides a deeper understanding of public sentiment. There is an opportunity for two-way learning that did not exist before.

Digital media changes the news cycle dramatically. This can work in your favour if you are focussed and responsive, allowing government to be focussed, topical and responsive. Of course, this can quickly backfire if the engagement strategy is too focussed on 'old-world' assumptions of top-down information delivery.

In summary, the benefits that digital engagement offers include:

- Scalable engagement done in short timeframes
- Strengthening existing relationships
- Reaching new audiences
- Tailored to the situation and audience
- An enabling process for citizens, giving them a greater sense of civic connectedness
- Cost savings, such as having applications created and data analysed by third-parties, better targeting of engagement and more efficient and effective policy outcomes.[42]

There are numerous strategies that can lead to a greater probability of success in online engagement. Ensuring that engagement is embedded within the processes and culture of the organisation matters. Engagement does not just happen as an afterthought or on the periphery, it works when it is fully integrated and this includes being open and listening. The biggest risk to organisational deafness is the inherent risk aversion of government agencies and a fear of exposing the organisation to the outside world. In fact, it is important to go beyond listening and become reflexive and responsive to internal and external feedback on the process itself so that it can be constantly refined and improved.

---

[42] Though the actual unit cost of engagement can be higher because greater resources are required. This is particularly true where the engagement exercise is multi-media or more extensive than traditional approaches.

A clear part of this is ensuring transparency and feedback. In other words, when you engage:[43]

BE CREDIBLE	Ensure the whole team is committed to engagement throughout the policy cycle. Encourage participation from enthusiastic individuals and teams; showcase their work internally to build commitment and awareness.
BE CONSISTENT	Encourage a range of people to get involved in discussions and ensure that you respond promptly to all questions or suggestions, providing feedback and information. Focus on developing good content; do not let the medium become the message.
BE RESPONSIVE	Play a role in the discussions taking place, outlining how participants' perspectives are feeding in to government deliberations. Diffuse conflicts and provide signposts to information, steering the discussion to focus on important topics. Allow audiences to use your content creatively, where possible.
BE INTEGRATED	Combine online and offline engagement, making sure that your approach and language suits the needs of the target communities. Decide whether you require large- or small-scale projects to get the best result, and make sure that staff time is properly allocated.
BE TRANSPARENT	Explain your position to people where relevant and update stakeholders about how decisions are being made. Be honest about what can be achieved, what is up for discussion and what is 'off topic'.

With the prevalence of social media and networked communities it is important to model the existing behaviour amongst your target audience. You can't force people to engage on your terms, especially when they are distrusting of you and disengaged from the process.

---

[43] Miller, L. & Williamson, A. (2008). Digital Dialogues Third Phase Report. London: Hansard Society/Ministry of Justice.

Consider ways to incentivise engagement. This can range from being appreciative and responsive of people giving their time and energy and making it clear what is in it for participants through to adopting some principles of gaming theory and gameplay that can provide direct incentives, rewards and even competitions for participants. Be yourself, remain authentic and be honest about your weaknesses and mistakes. People expect a certain voice and gravitas from a government agency, it is part of your brand, but that does not mean you can't be approachable and human!

Finally, target your audience proactively. Don't assume they will be interested and come to you. A key value of networks is the ability to create viral messages, leveraging this and the people you do engage with to spread the word and engage further.

Digital engagement works when there are clear objectives, careful planning, appropriate marketing and reflexive strategies for responding, managing and evaluating. Policy benefits, government departments see enhanced profiles and the public report greater trust in the political process and better understanding of government.

Thinking ahead, there is the potential to create new digital public commons which are co-managed by communities and governments as partnership models for information, engagement and discussion.

The key to this new phase of engagement platforms is in shared ownership and an effective orbit strategy. This refers to the need to make government (and democracy) 'sticky', to give people a reason to connect and stay connected. This can range from creating community to motivational tools such as competitions and league tables. The value of social media lies in this very approach but it's not original. This is what successful commercial brands have long been out to achieve: Nike, McDonalds, Amazon to name but three all build their offering around a direct relationship with you and one that you, the consumer aspire to maintain. Through this they build community and trust.

This is of course easy for a desirable consumer brand, it is a lot harder for government, particularly at a time when trust in public services and politicians remains low. The challenge therefore is to reverse this decline in interest and trust by using the strategies that clearly work elsewhere. Trust, for example, is about who you know: your level of trust is in large part determined by the recommendations of those in your social network (consider the power of ranking systems such as those at the core of eBay, Amazon and LastMinute.com).

Add to this landscape the development of cloud-based services, which are ideally suited for hosting shareable applications and data repositories, the increased interest in 'smart' cities and regions and the growth of gamification in social media spaces and we can see that the engagement landscape will continue to evolve.

Digital media can and does facilitate and mediate the creation of digital public spheres. E-participation is a formal relationship between citizens and government but social media enhances this by creating new, informal relationships amongst and between citizens and between citizens and government. Done well, this creates the space for us to 'do with' government. But this requires new thinking and new ways of engaging. Otherwise the old-world 'doing to' mind set will persist within government and any green shoots of nascent democratic renewal will wither.

Effective engagement is not simple. Social media creates opportunities for new democratic as well as social spaces but trust must be earned through our actions, not assumed or pre-ordained through traditional hegemonies.

Social media and the digital opportunities now in front of us can support transformation into a more citizen-centric, two-way society. But only if civil society is an active participant. We all need to be resourced to become active partners in our own future. Where government was a high-walled garden, the internet has built itself around people and their networks. Top down is not an effective model for effective engagement, nor is it an effective model for building trust.

> ❖ Digital lets us do democracy in our own space and time like never before.
>
> ❖ It's an opportunity to 'do with' people.
>
> ❖ It's a good place to connect people and build partnerships.
>
> ❖ It's an even better place to listen to what's going on.

The Weak Ties of Social Media

Networked democracy feels different for each of us. Our perceptions depend our own motivations but also on our sense of both the individual and collective benefit that derives from engaging in a network. Stronger identification with a particular community hopefully results in more political participation.[44] We've seen a reduction on levels of community cohesion and sentiment and with it a decrease in social relations and a decline in political participation. The once-strong social networks between citizens that encourage engagement have been eroded.

Let's think too about the nature of our community ties, the strong ties that exist amongst friends and family and the weak ties that exist between our acquaintances and members of civil society more widely.

As we move from the individual outwards, the strength of ties between citizens become weaker, representing multiple collections of acquaintances as opposed to the close-knit family group towards the centre of the diagram. Yet it is these weak ties that bring together otherwise disparate individuals around shared beliefs.[45] The power of weak ties highlights the importance of maintaining long term contact across social networks since it is in the maintenance of weak ties that social media is particularly effective.

---

[44] Rousseau, J-J. (2000), Du contrat social: Principes du droit politique. Ellipses: Paris
[45] Granovetter, M. (1985). Economic action and social structure: The problem of embeddedness. The American Journal of Sociology, Vol. 91, No. 3 (Nov., 1985), pp. 481-510

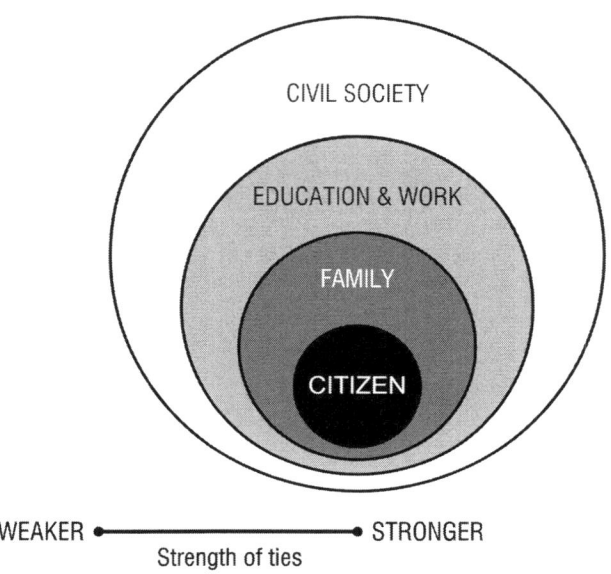

WEAKER ●————————————● STRONGER

Strength of ties

Effective online engagement presupposes a shift from the informational to the participatory. Both of these activities have been possible since the early days of the internet, using what are referred to as Web1.0 technology. And they remain firmly anchored in the internet landscape of today. Going beyond these we have now introduced concepts collectively known as Web 2.0, but more meaningfully referred to as the 'social' or 'user generated' web. This means websites and applications that are driven by two key factors: data provided by external third parties and the ability of tools to support interconnectivity and networking (not to mention a third, more subtle factor, the ability to monetise data; the user becomes the product).

Where online information repositories, Wikipedia and government engagement websites are firmly rooted in the Web 1.0 world, tools such as Facebook, Twitter and Four Square clearly align with the definitions of Web 2.0. Where value was previously derived from information (either providing or receiving) in a Web 2.0 world it lies in connecting – the building of weak ties and networks of association.

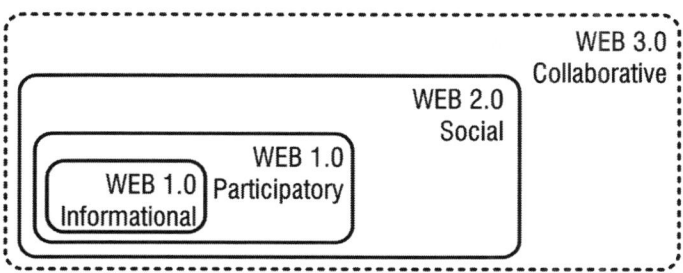

The next phase of evolution lies around the bringing together of formally instantiated data and user-driven data (and narrative) to power tools that rely on collaborative works. In part this can happen through the use of semantic searching and analysis techniques. An example of this was the work done by the Guardian newspaper to publish data sets for MPs expenses that the public could then access and in turn build up a collaborative analysis. The second facet of the collaborative web is to do with how we access the internet, moving from static single locations to always on, always with us mobile devices and applications – the future is data-enabled and mobile.

It is the power of user-generated content, collaboration and mobile that makes the internet a core tool for engagement. These tools are inherently focussed around the networks of association that hold people loosely together, making it easier for leaders to emerge and to motivate and connect with others in order to take action.

The internet is an ideal support tool for citizen engagement because of its viral, emergent, connected and rapid nature but is only a reflector of the society around it; it is only through the social appropriation of technology that it gains value. Today we are living in the midst of a global economic crisis. Whilst its impact and effect is more obvious in some European countries than in others, it none the less looms large as a spectre across the EU. It is also the rationale presented for the reduction in public spending. Public services are again subject to major review, reform and reconstruction, which in effect means deconstruction and outsourcing the delivery without the requisite funding. The UK's 'Big Society' represents a shift in ideological thinking that, its proponents claim, will reinvigorate local communities, reduce government bureaucracy and waste and put decision making powers back at the heart of citizenship. Opponents argue that it is a cynical attempt to cut expenditure (and therefore taxation), in effect cutting loose the most vulnerable with little or no safety net. It is hard to argue with the basic concepts of the 'big society'; many communities across Europe have for many years empowered themselves and taken action. Many have achieved great results but many too fail, either because they lack resources (money, people, time), because the system they are trying to change is so impenetrable, resistant and ultimately, unwilling to respond or because they have failed to generate the scale or the reach needed to achieve their ultimate goal.

Across the Middle East and North Africa we witnessed a rising tide of citizen-led protest against autocratic and corrupt regimes. In echoes of the Czech Spring of 1968 and the tumultuous wave of change that swept across Eastern Europe during the 1990s, there was a real feeling that change was real, could happen and that it could be sustained. This brought about a new and emergent spirit of pan-Arabism, with activists in one country following and gaining confidence (and support) from those in others. There is nothing new in this; we have seen such movements before during the 1960s and the 1980s. Some of the countries that rose up most recently were the same ones who were brutally repressed 50 years ago. The difference between then and now is the rise of digital media and a globalised 24x7 news culture. Unfortunately, as we've seen with the benefit of hindsight, this ignition of rapid change fails to deliver the desired transformation if all it manages to do is leave a power vacuum.

Key tools for the modern revolution are digital because they achieve significant things; first, they bring together otherwise remote and disparate groups. Second, they create channels to bypass traditional state control of the media so the outside world (in other words, foreign media) can see what is going on. Alongside traditional activism and action, the tools of the trade today are the internet (for information dissemination and news), social media (to connect and coordinate), mobile phones (to capture what happens) and digital, particularly satellite, television to report it. But they will fail if the social and structural processes aren't being put in place too.

The underlying complexity of the network is an important factor too. Whilst many regimes would like to simply turn off the internet, this is very difficult to do completely. Activists on the ground and net-savvy supporters around the world are able to implement proxy techniques to evade detection and bypass the controls of states. Flows of information can be slowed but not stopped; the world is now simply too porous. Images of war, disaster and violence regular flood our news media. However when they do, how often can be sure that the reporting is truly neutral and objective? How long is our interest maintained and how quickly is one war relegated to the back pages whilst another emergent disaster takes its place?

Social media is important because it is an ideal tool for connecting loose networks of association, bringing together otherwise disparate groups and individuals to support a common cause. It can also drive media attention and it is clearly no respecter of borders. What happens in Morocco and Egypt motivates and empowers protesters in Libya, Syria and Yemen. We saw digital activists from Morocco support Egyptians, teaching them how to exploit these new tools. One must be careful not to overstate the role of social media; it is only a tool. The previous example was largely done face-to-face, not online, and what social media can achieve is down to alignment with social behaviour and its effective social appropriation. That said, social media does play an important part in contemporary revolutionary movements; we saw around 40-45 tweets per minute from Egypt and 30-35 per minute from Syria and Libya at critical moments. The warning, however, is obvious given recent history: social media does nothing in the long term and change fails if your plans aren't ready to put in place. When power falters other, less democratic, but better organised groups take advantage and step into the void.

Twitter receives much media attention, perhaps because it is more visible to the media. Therein lies its value, as a tool to tell your story to the world. This is reflected in the significant number of tweets in English, particularly from Egypt at the time of the Tahrir Square occupation. Equally Facebook's role in Egypt and across North Africa was to show a growing mass public that they were not alone; suddenly an emerging pan-Arab movement for change was made visible on their social networks, from where individual citizens quickly took courage and then action.

Facebook has proven a key tool for collaboration and network-formation, Twitter for coordinating action quickly in real time and both Twitter and YouTube provide a documented public record for the outside world.

Perhaps most telling is that the use of social networking sites such as Facebook to organise and promote demonstrations is now mentioned in passing, almost casually by those involved. What we saw in North Africa mirrors what we saw in Germany and the UK during recent elections. First, a media wanting to portray social media as being more important than it really is but, more importantly, clear evidence that the internet – blogs, Facebook, Twitter, Instagram and more; citizen journalism and the consumption of these – is simply becoming normative: it is business as usual, at least it is amongst a significant cohort in terms of scale (UK and Germany) and influence (Egypt and Libya). But none of this means that it is the game changer that some people would have us believe it could be.

- ❖ We have strong ties amongst friends and family and weak ties between our acquaintances and wider networks.
- ❖ People trust people who actively listen to them.
- ❖ Strong ties are great catalysts for action, weak ties are powerful connectors to build momentum quickly.
- ❖ Social media is highly effective at building and maintaining weak ties.
- ❖ Social media doesn't replace good planning and power vacuums form if you are not prepared for change.
- ❖ Citizen journalism and the use of mobile is a critical reporting tool in crises and conflicts, just as it should be in the local town hall.

Embedding Digital Advantage

Of course, digital is only any use if everyone who wants to use it can use it. Digital deficit is a reality everywhere, to a greater or lesser degree. As we've said, digital is not a panacea and one critical reason for this is that it leaves behind those who lack access to it, the ability or desire to use it or the skills to be an effective user. There are many reasons for being offline but it is sufficient to point out that you are less likely to have the internet if you are old, poor, poorly educated, have a disability or live in a remote rural area. Beyond this, there appears to be a distinct gender gap in the political life of many countries. Of itself, digital does nothing to address this.[46] Five primary barriers to access in this context can include:[47]

- Mental access – A lack of interest, motivation or anxiety.
- Material access – The inability to obtain access to technology.
- Skills access – Lack of 'digital' skills.
- Usage access – Lack of significant usage opportunities.
- Democratic access – Unable to harness digital tools for political participation or to influence.

---

[46] Williamson, A. (2011, Sep 1). The gender imbalance online seems to be the result of wider political exclusion, not digital exclusion. British Politics and Policy at LSE. London School of Economics.

[47] Hacker, K. L., & van Dijk, J. (2000). What is digital democracy? In J. v. Dijk & K. L. Hacker (Eds.), Digital democracy: Issues of theory and practice (pp. 1-9). London Thousand Oaks, CA: SAGE; Norris, P. (2001). Digital Divide. Cambridge, UK: Cambridge University Press.

Digital is valuable when it can be used effectively. It extends traditional concepts of media into an interactive experience where the views of many can be expressed and potentially, disseminated widely. It extends the experience to support (and encourage) discourse (thought of themselves, digital applications have not proven particularly effective as discursive tools). It's this potential to reach out and to bring people together that sets digital tools apart from traditional print and electronic media. It is this which offers us the greatest potential for citizens to become more involved in the political and democratic processes, even though that process is not necessarily carried out entirely online.

The internet has fragmented and decentralised the context in which communication occurs such that 'experts' must compete with unedited egalitarian sources of information: it has given us the opportunity to democratise information and knowledge.[48] Though with this comes an increased need to assess the veracity of the information presented.

But all is not equal online and there's a need for a framework to manage the mis-match between policy and the grounded and community use of digital tools. Policy, and those charged with executing it are consistently seen to be out of touch with what's happening in our communities almost as much as we're out of touch with what they're doing!

The framework in this chapter underpins a lot of the detailed work that needs to happen to build active democracies. It provides a baseline for digital advantage and effective participation. It bridges the more strategic and tactical examples with actual community based-initiatives, acknowledging that:

---

[48] Habermas, J. (2006). Ein avantgardistischer spürsinn für relevanze: Was den intellektuellen auszeichnet. Wien, Austria: Renner Institut.

1. Access and literacy are societal issues so must be addressed at a policy level.
2. Partnerships allow active communities to work together in formal and informal ways.
3. Partnerships can realise economies of scale, bring on board funding or provide specialist skills and training that would otherwise not be available to the community.
4. Within communities, projects require visionaries to lead them and skills development to ensure that, once projects become established and operationalized, resources and momentum exist to sustain them.

We've identified five stages of maturity for the use of digital within communities (and beyond), which can be used as both an assessment tool (for current maturity) and as a planning or policy development tool.

1. Access
2. Literacy
3. Content
4. Creation
5. Dissemination

Each of the five stages recognises an increasing maturity and sophistication in the use of digital. However, the model isn't linear: the target is not to reach 'stage five', rather that technology is being applied in a way that is seen as appropriate to the community in question at a point in time (either present or future) across all the stages. In this model, stages 1 through to 4 occur within our communities and organisations. They are not necessarily formal and are not entirely dependent on each other.

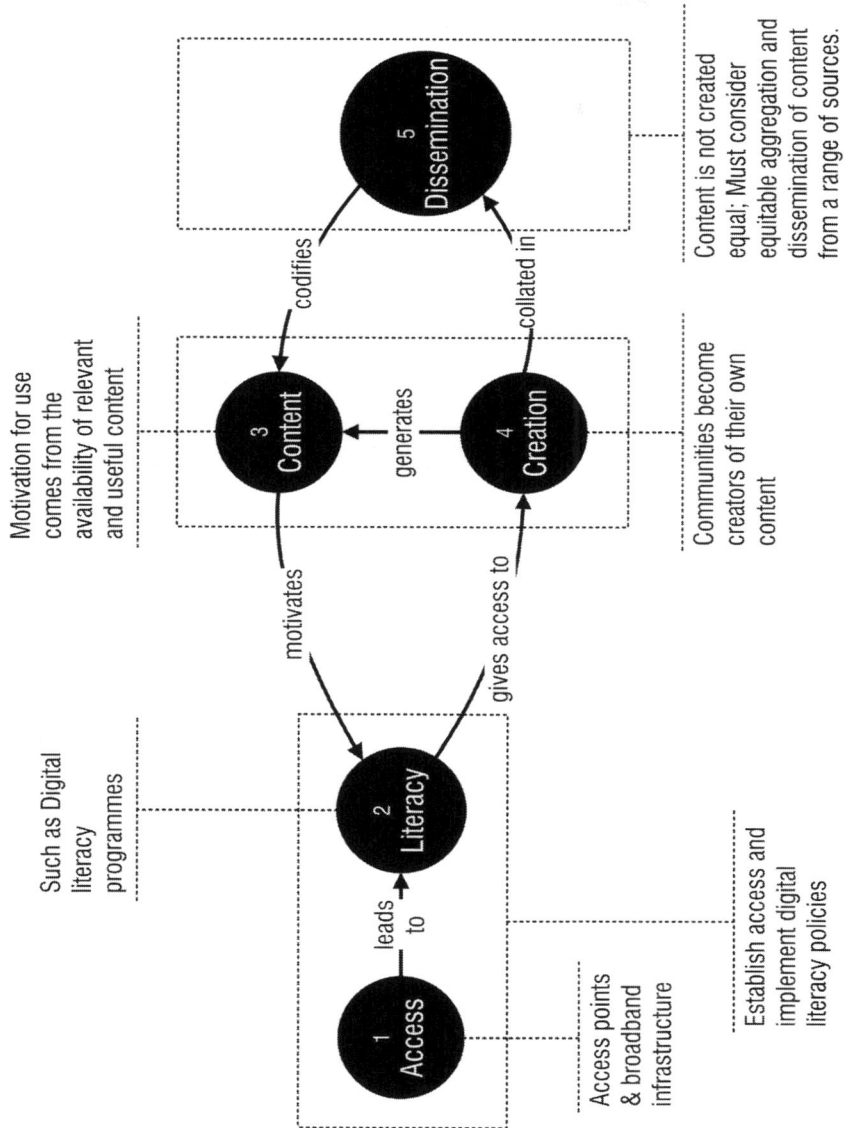

Motivation for use comes from the availability of relevant and useful content

Such as Digital literacy programmes

Content is not created equal; Must consider equitable aggregation and dissemination of content from a range of sources.

Communities become creators of their own content

Establish access and implement digital literacy policies

Access points & broadband infrastructure

5 Dissemination

3 Content

4 Creation

2 Literacy

1 Access

codifies

collated in

generates

motivates

gives access to

leads to

STAGE 1 – ACCESS	It is not lack of access which causes a digital deficit but the consequences of that lack of connection.[49] Hence strategies are required to ensure equity of access and opportunity. Citizens must have basic access to good broadband, the hardware to connect and the tools to use.
STAGE 2 – LITERACY	People in communities need training and support to make effective use of digital (from basic internet skills to analytical understanding of open data).
STAGE 3 – CONTENT	For digital tools to be useful and for communities to be motivated to use them, material and services must be available online that are of a perceived value to the community. Communities need to be aware of these tools and have access to them.
STAGE 4 – CREATION	Communities at this stage have the knowledge, skills and facilities necessary to produce and publish information themselves and to re-package or highlight information that is directly pertinent to them. This could be community forums or Facebook, the best tool is the one that suits the community, never one that's been imposed by someone else.
STAGE 5 – DISSEMINATION	The final stage is a meta-stage, occurring on or beyond individual community boundaries. As communities become publishers of new knowledge, we risk becoming overwhelmed with information. Some information is more readily available and accessible than others; because the producer is more widely known or because of search engine bias. In a truly participative society, we have to ensure fair and equitable dissemination of information (being received at Stage 3 and created at Stage 4). Meta data and open data repositories are examples of how this can work.

---

[49] Castells, M. (2001). The Internet galaxy: Reflections on the Internet, business, and society. New York: Oxford University Press.

The requirements and relative importance of a stage is related to the maturity of use. In other words, each of the four stages, whilst to some degree reliant on its predecessor, does not require that prior stages were formalised or even articulated. We've seen a range of situations from a laissez-faire approach through to formal strategy or policy initiatives.

Let's contextualise this model by looking at Peter Day's three components of community technology: Policy, partnerships and practice[50], and cross-mapping Stage 1, Access:

POLICY	Local government affirms that digital skills are a basic life skill and commits to citizens having access to broadband internet as close to home as possible. This is implemented as an information access strategy that places internet-enabled computers in local libraries, council offices and even subsidises the use of Wi-Fi in local cafes.
PARTNERSHIPS	Hosts are required for sites; obvious partners are council and libraries. However, at this level the project has no community buy-in or ownership so the concept can be extended to include local community groups that already use the facilities. Partnerships become more significant as maturity increases.
PRACTICE	If the technology is supported by the host, then little is required at this level; the technology could be passive and available for passive users. However, it is likely that more effective use could be achieved if local community members become proactive, perhaps creating groups, such as for senior citizens (where the peer-support can be used to break down technology barriers).

[50] Day, P. (2004b). Community (information and communication) technology: Policy, partnership and practice. In S. Marshall, W. Taylor & Y. Xinghuo (Eds.), Using Community Informatics to Transform Regions (pp. 18-36). Melbourne, VIC: Idea Group.

And viewed from the perspective of each stage within the five-stage model, the importance of a forward-looking policy agenda becomes obvious:

ACCESS AND LITERACY	Driven by policy and potentially funded as a result, however, this often requires partnerships to acquire external expertise; localized delivery is an important success factor, meaning that community-based practitioners are required to actualize the policy. As already suggested, access and literacy strategies are important for disadvantaged or marginalized communities.
CONTENT AND CREATION OF CONTENT	Partnerships can provide technology, skills and opportunity (for example, community-based hosting projects); local practitioners are required to drive the creation of content.
COLLATION AND DISSEMINATION OF LIKE RESOURCES	As communities reach levels of digital and online maturity, partnerships become vital to ensure equitable distribution and recognition of local content. Potential projects include geographic portals that can be beyond the resource capability of a single community and hence the availability of external funding partners becomes a critical success factor at this stage.

❖ Digital is only useful if people have access and the skills to use it.

❖ We have to ensure we're not creating a new digital elite.

❖ Digital equality must be addressed at a policy level: the internet as a right.

❖ Content is not created equally so we have to curate community knowledge and ensure effective aggregation and dissemination.

Education is a Critical Component

Effective use of digital requires digital literacy but to get involved in democracy in an effective way, we need to go a lot further, we need information and political literacy too.

How is one supposed to participate when systems remain opaque, difficult to navigate and distant from our everyday lives? The answer lies partly in technology but this is only a tool - an enabler. Technology alone cannot make a difference, only how we use it can. And to be able to use it effectively we require sufficient knowledge of the democratic and governmental systems and sufficient skills to be able to manage, review and form opinions based on a vast array of data. We need core skills in political literacy and information literacy.

The formal education system has on the whole done a poor job of equipping our newest democratic citizens with either of these skills. In the UK, political literacy education is poor and rather disparate. It appears that we place more value in history (the past) than political literacy (the future). Whilst both are important (you cannot deliver a new future without understanding the past), the current system ensures low levels of engagement.

This problem is historical too, so it is not just the young but many others who remain poorly informed about democracy. All of this can be rectified by the provision of easy to follow information where people are – libraries, community centres, through civil society groups and schools.

For those who feel they lack the knowledge to take part in democracy, we need to create opportunities for embedded learning. This can come as part of other training, through lifelong learning courses, through more informal ways of learning and knowledge gathering and peer-to-peer knowledge exchange. Through these methods of education, citizens can build up the skills that enable participation, including an increased level of knowledge and awareness, increased confidence and self-esteem and an awareness of the benefit of participation.

It looks something like this framework for engagement:

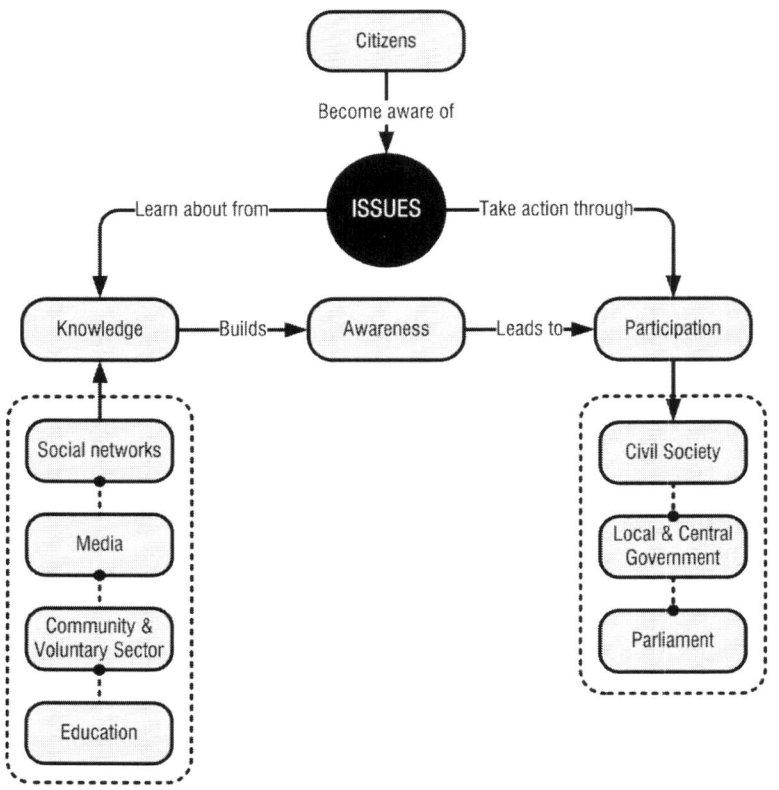

The knowledge component of the framework is built up through membership of social networks, consumption of the media, through intervention from the community and voluntary sector and through traditional methods of education. It is both formal and informal.

❖ Everyone has the right to engage in their own future.

❖ Political and information literacy are both vital components of a modern society.

❖ We need just-in-time learning for people who want to get involved in democracy.

❖ We learn from our networks, knowledge increases awareness and awareness leads us to participate more.

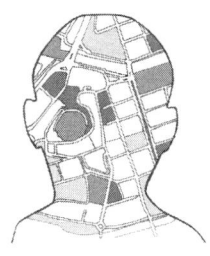

A Framework for
Transformation

.

Co-creating Order From Disorder

People have to feel needed… We don't always offer people a purpose. When people feel there is a purpose and that they're needed, there's not much else to do except let them do the work
– Maya Angelou

So far we've described how we see the landscape, both the past and what we believe the future needs to look like. We've highlighted some of the things that we see as the barriers to creating a better, more active, democracy and we've brought in the role of digital, which we believe is a critical (but not the only) enabler.

If we have to summarise where we're at it's that digital matters, that conversations matter and building real connections matter. It's that networks are critical for building active democracies and that we need as many people as possible to actively participate in those networks. We believe that power has to be shared and co-created ideas can resonate much more powerfully. We know that we don't have all the answers (we don't even have all the questions!). That's why we want to make this book a catalyst for conversations to help us all design, create and sustain new forms of active democracies. In this section we want to talk about what you can do to start building a culture and a practice of active democracy. How you can start and lead a co-creative, innovative and transformative process to make democracy work better for more people.

Democracy fundamentally works to let us achieve order and to re-create orderliness, which is rather ironic given that our frustrations with it are leading to increasing disorder. Control and arrogance impose solutions promoted by the few that are not mandated, accepted or even understood by the many. Power, as we discussed earlier, is dispersed in and throughout societies but it is concentrated in the hands of a few. The consequence is an increased challenge to the legitimacy of this power to create, decide and realise our futures. The rules of the game have changed. Failing to recognise this, to continue as before, creates a pattern of actions that are quickly seen as controlling and arrogant. When so-called disorder emerges to challenge the misuse of power, the powerful look for corrective actions to recreate the order they expect and desire. Politicians might criticise the supposed power of the media yet they have cynically "tried to bend it to their own purpose"[51]. Though, despite the rhetoric, it was never really The Sun "wot won it" for Tony Blair in 1997.[52]

We look for new solutions to evolve and re-balance democracy.

As we see it, we have lost the art of collaboration. Yet collaboration is exactly what we need to do if we are to engage and work with the complexity of our modern societies. Collaboration and co-creation is at the heart of active democracies. So we are asking the question: how will representative democracy become capable of addressing our social sustainability challenges when the rules of the game have changed so fundamentally?

What seems to be happening is a shift from the (narrow) state to the (whole) nation as the essential part of creating order and managing complexity and resolving conflict points. Previously such things have

---

[51] The Power Inquiry. (2006). Power to the people. York: Joseph Rowntree Charitable Trust & Joseph Rowntree Reform Trust.
[52] Curtice, J. (1999). Was it the Sun wot won it again? The influence of newspapers in the 1997 election campaign. Oxford: Centre for Research into Social Trends

also been managed within the boundaries of single nation-states, within the decision-making power of that nation and the legitimacy of elected officials. Now and going forward it seems more challenging and less rational to use geographical borders as a logical system level of decision-making. The multi-layer governance models that nations today operate under fuel the complexity and dilute elected officials power, spreading power within and beyond the system. Power is everywhere and nowhere at the same time, as Hans Abrahamsson, researcher in peace and global studies, observes.[53]

However, the emerging complexity and the emerging patterns of conflict that are portrayed in today's societies make it necessary to acknowledge and act upon a different set of rules, ones that operate on several levels at the same time. For example, a nation like Sweden in its governance model is not only able to act within the national boundaries but has to take into account globalization, legislation and legal charters from the European Union and multi-national organisations too, such as the United Nations and World Trade Organisation.

This is perhaps too big an issue for us to describe in sufficient detail in a single chapter of a small book. However, we would like to focus on the ability of a nation "to create orderliness" in the context of today. How is ordered created? How is predictability created? Before, when life operated at a lower level of complexity, conflicts where managed in and between political parties. There was a concentration of power to elected officials. One could say that they were in control. In times of instability order was recreated by emitting force and decisions made from a foundation of assumed legitimacy and acceptance. Maybe it is an illusion but it seems that the emergence of new ways of communicating and interacting have caused a new pattern to emerge.

---

[53] Abrahamsson, H. (2013). Power and dialogue in just and socially sustainable Swedish cities. Concept paper for SALAR and SSSDSC. Available at: www.mistraurbanfutures.org/sites/default/files/power_and_dialogue_-_12.10.2013.pdf

Traditionally in Sweden the social contract is seen as being very strong, hence citizens place their trust in and expect the state to take care of them, to maintain the social order. Elected officials and civil servants, Swedes believe, are professionals and so they legitimate power from this logic. But what we see today seems to be a counter intuitive behaviour in decision making. Citizen's trust in politicians is declining, the desire to be engaged in the current ways of expressing political ambitions fails to attract members to parties. The citizens seem to expect from their elected officials a level of clarity and decisiveness when making complex and tough decisions. Yet when this decision making power is used in cutting costs that affect people, citizen's protest and obstruct those decisions. They are dis-trusting and no longer see either the decision makers or the decisions as legitimate. It seems like a 'Catch 22' and is certainly not a phenomenon that is limited to Sweden. Suddenly order is neither established by or contained in formal society. So far this seems to work well enough, tough decisions are pushed through despite a resistant public opinion, and, when the dust settles, voices go silent. How long this can continue we would not like to speculate but it seems to us to be an untenable position to maintain. There must be limits to this pattern of protest followed by (perhaps frustrated) silence? Are these constant waves of disappointment and resignation dissipating or does the half-life of discontent build up such that at some point social unrest emerges? Will extremist views and the parties that espouse them gain more traction and interest from voters? We are already seeing this across parts of Europe. Support comes not perhaps because the extremists have widespread public support but because they are seen as an alternative to the status quo, who it is perceived have let us down. Recent opinion polls in Sweden suggest a distinctive shift of support towards the far right of the political spectrum.

How is our democratic energy channelled today? In Sweden the Law of Referendums was changed in 2011. Now, if 10% of the population sign a petition and one-third of the City Council votes for it, a referendum must be held. During 2013 and 2014, Sweden held 26 of these. The absolute majority are reactions to decisions that have already been made. So "resistance" has perfectly adequate channels to voice its opposing opinion. Facebook groups are created and populated with likes in days, and sometimes hours if the topic is "hot" enough.

How is the opinion storm managed by officials? How does it influence the decisions and decision makers? Does it? Is being a politician today to "act in the market" of raised voices, promoting am unwavering view? The landscape of political decisions is like geyser, ready to explode! But who really is in control, on whose mandate? Is there a pattern that delivers to those who are able to shout the loudest, have the deepest pockets to lobby or are already part of the inner elite? In these settings, power emerges and then disappears but without citizens being able to take responsibility or ensure accountability. All too often we abdicate responsibility, happy enough to leave the politicians to take the tough decisions. Not trusting them and yet actively resisting when it comes to close. Not in my backyard but neither is it my job to make the decision!

A Swedish survey on civic engagement showed that 66% of the population want to take part in activities to co-create society when invited to by their local municipality. Only 4% were prepared to start protest groups.[54] So maybe the volatile, geyser like landscape we're experiencing today is a symptom of our frustration at not being able to realise our desire to co-create? Maybe the civic unrest we see so much of today is the consequence of the frustration that emerges when a lack of connection, transparency and interactivity permeate our democracies? The energy and desire to co-create is there, but we need to co-create the process for engagement, the infrastructure for

---

[54] See: j.mp/SKLCivicEngagement

influence and invite people in to the heart of our decision making processes.

The patterns of complexity and necessity for making the tough decisions that lie ahead of us require us to collectively re-energise democracy towards a model of co-creation and intimacy. We need to build places where power, responsibility and accountability are shared. Unfortunately we don't seem to be on a path heading in that direction. We need to recognise that we are in a new world, where order is not created through the old ways. In order to create active democracies, we've got to establish some core principles:

1. Trust-building is the primary objective for our process design and interactions.
2. Serious co-transformation work needs to involve many stakeholders.
3. Accept the complexity and become active learners.
4. Co-creation is a relationship, sharing both power and responsibility.
5. Actively exploring conflicts of interest means actively surfacing alternative views to enrich wisdom and create energy to act out of respect and trust.
6. Opening up to co-creation has to happen sooner rather than later, particularly when dealing with complex issues and trade-offs.
7. We achieve more if we start with prototypes, learn from failure and enshrine active learning.

- ❖ Democracy is a process of co-creating order in our society.
- ❖ Complexity has got in the way and allowed the system to break down.
- ❖ We need to understand how we can effectively channel democratic energy.
- ❖ Who really has a mandate to make decisions that affect our lives?

Re-energising Democracy

Our own research and practice show us that to become engaged in a democratic process citizens have to first value the core tenets of an active democracy and become motivated to pursue a democratic agenda. We (you, me, the government, politicians) can't tell anyone to get involved in democracy – they have to believe in the value of engagement. This is a personal journey played out by each of us in society.

Being an active participant in democracy is a choice and to choose to take part you must trust the process and believe that it (and the people in it) has efficacy. Active democracies and active networks in those democracies can act as catalysts for engagement but we need more, we need to see personal value in participation.

Even though new digital methods are often proposed as a solution to disengagement and to enhancing participation, they remain only tools. The focus must be on the benefits to people and not on the technological aspects. Generating awareness, and subsequently trust, requires simple messages.

We want you to create an effective co-transformative model of democracy, one which is simultaneously grounded in the values and aspirations of the community, serves as an effective decision making tool and is flexible and responsive enough to use the right tools at the right time. To help focus your thinking on what this looks like and what it means, let's consider seven critical attributes that are needed for active democracies.

Social sphere

The 'social sphere' refers to the human side of democracy. This is where we build awareness about the underlying tools and processes, what they are and how they work. It's the space in which we promote deliberative models and make them accessible to everyone, as well as defining and promoting the roles of both community and government:

> **Awareness** of what can be done.

> **Deliberation**, the process of more effective civic engagement in democratic practices and the barriers to this that exist.

> **Grounded leadership** comes from those who are aware of the potential and can promote new ideas, advocating and leading change. Conversely, such 'leaders' can inhibit uptake by failing to communicate effectively or by maintaining the status quo.

This requires a level of leadership both from inside and outside formal organisations. Look for emergent leaders who can build networks, share ideas and bring people together. Look for new ways to convene, work and convey outcomes. Look to harness the best technologies that you have – face-to-face meetings, pen and paper, digital and social media.

Technical sphere

Beneath but supporting the social sphere is a technical sphere that relates to the application of digital tools and processes; these are the processes that govern the use of your technology and the solutions that technology supports and, potentially, enhances:

Digital itself, its effective use and adoption and issues relating to digital uptake, including inequity and barriers to adoption.

Process, or what has to happen to transform, change and support processes; who is responsible for this and what barriers or resistance exist.

Solutions (projects and initiatives) that link technology to process but also recognise, at the strategic level, the importance of sustainability and scalability.

Transformative praxis

Change is socially driven. In the case of active democracies – or more accurately co-transformational democracy in the early stages – change occurs through the alignment of the adoption of new technologies with changing social processes. The key transformative attribute of emergent technologies is disruption.

Disruption of current processes and power structures leading to opportunities for new processes and solutions enabled by new tools, new methods, new mind sets and more (new) people to emerge.

Transformative praxis is the link between the social and the technical and provides the space for reclaiming [social] power in order to implement new [technical] solutions. The significance of these attributes is that changes (new or modified strategies, processes, systems) occur in the *technical* sphere through a *transformative* process that originates in the ideas and actions taking place in the *social* sphere (through awareness-building and advocacy). The *social* sphere is linked to the *technical* sphere through *transformative praxis*.

These attributes and their inter-relationships are represented diagrammatically below and can be described as follows:

- Grounded leadership
    - Promotes **awareness** of the potential for democratic change;
    - Advocates for and causes **disruption** to **transform** existing **processes**;
    - Facilitates the co-design, creation and deployment of new **processes**.
- Building **Awareness** amongst citizens
    - Increases **participation** in **deliberative** settings;
    - Promotes access to and the use [adoption] of **Digital**.
- **Digital** supports
    - The delivery of systems that instantiate new transformative processes.
- New **processes** and **systems** enable
    - The emergence of new models for deliberative engagement.

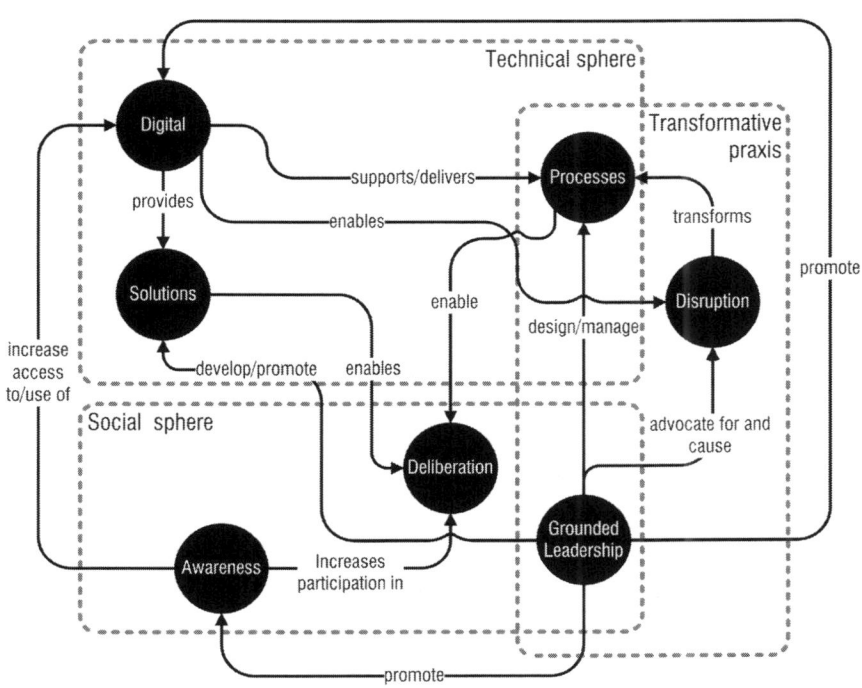

A Framework for Transformation

- ❖ Democracy is a personal journey – we all have to find our own value in it.
- ❖ We need to build awareness of what can be done.
- ❖ Digital tools can connect people who want to create and lead change.
- ❖ Networked democracy can create momentum and energise people.
- ❖ Grounded leadership brings people together and connects different groups.

A Framework for Transformation

Bridging the Strategic and the Tactical

Unfortunately re-building a 'fit-for-purpose' democracy is far from simple. There are significant barriers to change and the potential to perpetuate existing hegemonies and power-elites, even in new spaces, is high. Active democracy must by its very nature be ubiquitous so barriers to ubiquity must be identified and addressed. They can be technical, economic, cultural, social and political. To highlight the risk, adding a digital component to democratic engagement seems logical but it can create new barriers, particularly if people start believing the technology is determining the processes or that it undermines what it should be supporting. This is particularly the case where tools, digital or otherwise, are imposed on us and where we are forced to use a particular tool or method to engage. Imposing wrong, clumsy or inappropriate tools on citizens will see them quickly drift away. Digital is always a means to an end and never an end in itself, believing otherwise is always dangerous!

Digital tools prove valuable when they are harnessed along with other media for communicating a message. However they also extend the traditional concepts of media into an interactive and social experience, where the views of many can be expressed, expanded upon and disseminated widely. It is this potential that sets digital tools apart from traditional print and electronic media and which offers the greatest potential for citizens to become more involved in the political and democratic processes.

There is, though, a need for a clear framework to manage the explosion of new options, opportunities and tools. This is highlighted by the often-cited mis-match between strategy or policy and operational initiatives. Policy, and those charged with executing it, is consistently seen as being out of touch with what is happening in the community, in our real lives.

As part of an active democracy model, we need to consider an overarching framework that bridges the strategic and the tactical to align them with actual community based-initiatives. We need to do this in a way that promotes good practice and does not stifle innovation. Over the forthcoming chapters we're going to develop this model in more detail. What we hope you'll see is how it needs to be aligned with citizen-centric governance frameworks and designed to allow sustainable community-based democratic solutions to emerge. Though there is no perfect model for active democracies, any successful framework is likely to include:

1. Access (to tools and technology) and literacy (of technology and democracy) are societal issues so must be addressed at a macro or policy level.
2. Partnerships allow active communities to work together in either formal or informal ways.
3. Partnerships can be used to realise economies of scale, bring on board funding or to provide specialist skills or training that would otherwise not be available to the community.
4. Networks can be used to connect, energise and channel the concerns, views and actions of many people.
5. Within a community, projects require visionaries to lead the practice-side and skills development initiatives to ensure that, once projects become established and operationalized, localised resource and sufficient momentum exists to sustain them.

Active democracies need a strategy and a vision, so how do we go about developing this given the complexity and volatility of our modern society? We're all familiar with forecasting – projecting what we know today forward to, in effect, guess what might happen tomorrow. Democracy and politics are full of forecasts. Economic, political, technological, you name it. The problem is that we all too often build into these forecasts our baggage, biases and pre-conceptions. All too often, forecasts are simply history projected forward. But, as we've already said, the past is not a valid model for the democracies we need in the future.

We like to turn this problem around and 'backcast'.

Backcasting means deciding where we want to be and working backwards to put the actions in place today, so we can get there tomorrow. Perhaps it's not quite that simple but it is a way to overcome ingrained resistance, bias and siloed thinking.

To start this process we need to see a new future. We need a vision. And rather than work on a consensus so innocuous no one can possibly disagree, our suggestion is to get everyone involved in the issue to co-create multiple scenarios. These are big-picture ideal outcomes: what the future looks like for the participants in the process.

Scenarios are developed through a group process and they break the connection between the past, the present and the future. They allow everyone in the process to agree what the world looks like in three, five or even fifty years.

There can (and quite likely will) be multiple scenarios but these should always be high-level. There's no need to get bogged down in the detail because, if you succeed, the detail will be resolved along the way.

So, with backcasting, the end is the place to start.

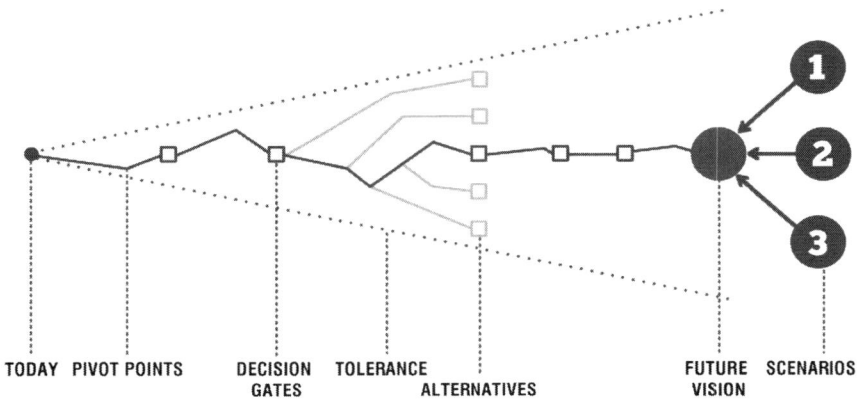

TODAY PIVOT POINTS   DECISION   TOLERANCE   FUTURE   SCENARIOS
GATES   ALTERNATIVES   VISION

❖ Democracy is too complex to change without a road-map.

❖ We have to link the big-picture to what happens every day.

❖ Part of the process involves a sustainable framework for
   community (devolved) decision making.

❖ Forecasting is pointless when change is rapid (you're wrong
   before you start), so start at the goal and work backwards
   without worrying about the detail.

❖ Pivot as you go and always be ready to change the plan if it
   isn't working.

❖ Innovate in small, rapid cycles then review, refresh and re-
   align.

❖ Partnerships create momentum, widen the knowledge and skills
   and break down silos.

Why Personal Engagement Matters

Active democracies are anchored in our communities and our networks so, to make our communities equal partners, we first have to privilege a range of advocacy, awareness-building and disruptive practices to initiate and sustain transformation. Grounded leaders can spark disruptive spaces so alternative discourses arise. These are the new centres of partnership, not power. These are the places where co-creation happens and trust begins to emerge. Either physical or virtual, and often both, they include underground publishing, social software and community meetings. They are formal and informal, planned and spontaneous, structured and unstructured.

So far we have focussed on the system and the process. All of this matters but all the way through this discussion we have talked about individuals at the heart of active, networked democracies.

There is a personal journey here too, because democracy is personal. We need good role models for active democracy, grounded leaders whom we trust. Here we need to explore how our model of engagement recognises individual motivations and how we adopt constantly changing roles as projects emerge, mature and conclude and processes develop, embed and fall away again. To do this we're focussing primarily on the social sphere and its relationship to the nature of transformative praxis. For now we're assuming that the technical sphere is a supporting player.

We're going to take two existing models, merge them together to mix things up and then re-position them to help you understand how individuals can both act in and influence active democracy. Most importantly we're going to establish a pattern of understanding that it is not simply what we do but when we do it that matters.

The two theoretical models taken together offer us a fresh way to look at engagement that is communally orientated and technologically agnostic. These are the Transtheoretical Model of Change[55] and Bill Moyer's lifecycle for social movements.[56] Combining these models provides a framework in which to locate the key social and community attributes of active democracy and this results in a process-oriented way of understanding the ways in which democracy and action transform both individually and collectively.

The Transtheoretical Model of Change, which is often implemented as Motivational Interviewing, emerged from decision-making theory and motivational psychology. This incorporates a trans-theoretical model of the stages of change, which act as a central construct around which individuals can modify behaviour. Originally this model was focussed on overcoming addictive behaviours (which is not as far from the old world model of democracy as you might think!). The model includes a series of independent variables referring to both the process of change which must occur as well as a series of related outcome measures. In our variation on the model, these stages of change will be used to define the key stages of awareness and process maturity in an active democracy and the associated individual engagement.

[55] Prochaska, J. O., & DiClemente, C. C. (1984). Toward a comprehensive model of change. In W. R. Miller & N. Heather (Eds.), Treating Addictive Behaviors: Processes of Change (pp. 3-27). New York: Plenum Press; Prochaska, J. O., & Velicer, W. F. (1997). The transtheoretical model of health behavior change. American Journal of Health Promotion(12), 38–48.

[56] Moyer, B. (2001). Doing democracy: The MAP model for organizing social movements. Gabriola Island, BC: New Society Publishers.

PRE-CONTEMPLATION	The person is not aware or not yet ready to consider that change is needed.
CONTEMPLATION	There is some awareness of the necessity (or desire) to change but resistance and ambivalence remains.
PREPARATION	At this stage people have become receptive to change and are actively considering how to make the changes needed.
ACTION	Actors are now engaged with making changes and adopting new ways of being or doing.
MAINTENANCE	The changes are complete and new ways are now maintained.

Traditional change models focus on influencing social norms, the Transtheoretical Model is based on individual motivation and intent – it's about you and me! It's this that we feel makes it appropriate for grass-roots engagement because it lets us accept resistance to systemic pressures to change and relies instead on our own motivation and how we value the process or desired outcome. It's a key principle of motivational interviewing that the focus is on individual engagement when the individual is ready, rather than when the system wants to force change (so ultimately we are diffusing power out to citizens to choose how and when to engage).

But motivation and awareness extends to the general population too. It encompasses government officers, politicians, civil society groups and activists. In the early stages of transformation, it is the citizen activists, and their internal innovative equivalents we talked about in the earlier chapter on 'Moving from arrogance to intimacy', that provide the kind of 'grounded leadership' we're looking for.

These are the rebels, already motivated by a need to change, open to new ideas and – to some degree at least – resourced to make change happen. They can lead us into new spaces as existing structures are challenged and new processes emerge. They are the catalysts for active democracy. There's nothing new here, this mirrors the traditional life-cycle of social movements that Moyer describes identifying four roles:[57]

- Reformer
- Rebel
- Citizen
- Change-agent

He suggests each of these roles is needed to create and sustain social movements that work effectively. Social movements must be seen as responsible citizens by the wider public. Yet at the same time, rebels must be willing to protest against established policies and social conditions, speaking out and voicing that all is not well.

The catalytic points here exist on the edge. Can the rebels in our communities raise the profile, raise the issues, and develop a coherent position so others can join and take them forward? There is a clear social innovation life cycle implicit in all of this. And it's remarkably similar to the one we see in technological innovation. Innovators need to find early adopters to champion their ideas but the real challenge comes when you attempt to reach out to a wider public. This is the 'early majority' you need to create sufficient mass, but they lack the passion and convictions of the early adopters and so become harder to reach and harder to engage with. It makes sense then that much innovation (technological and social) fails at this stage because it can't jump across the 'chasm' that exists between niche exclusivity and mainstream awareness and populism.[58]

What this tells us rather starkly is that the rebels working alone will fail. They will, in fact, always fail unless they or someone else can

---

[57] Moyer, B. (2001). Doing democracy: The MAP model for organizing social movements. Gabriola Island, BC: New Society Publishers.p.84.
[58] Moore. G.A. (1991). Crossing the chasm. New York: Harper Collins.

adapt. The rebel lacks the strategic skills and the process-oriented thinking that is needed to actually create and lead change. They lack the knowledge of the network and often even the access to that network. They can even lack the credibility, power and social acceptability to create a wider appetite for change. So for mainstream adoption to happen we need to find change-agents. These are the people who can craft the message, connect the wider networks and they can educate and organise the public to become aware of the issues. Change agents are the advocates for change and are supported by the reformers, who work with them to generate the real change and apply it to practice. Of course, change agents and reformers can emerge from within the ranks of the rebels, our roles are fluid and evolving!

> **Rebels** raise the flag and create the energy, **change-agents** harness this energy constructively and the **reformers** integrate new ideas back into the mainstream for **citizens** to use.

Egypt makes a classic, if depressing, case-study in what happens when passion escalates change ahead of organisation and planning. It is a clear example of where the change agents and reformers were overtaken by others more organised than themselves, poised to take advantage of the disruption. It warns us that there is old-world power around as we lead change and this will attempt to fill any vacuum you leave. The more radical the transformation we seek, the more contestable and potentially dangerous it becomes.

The Occupy movement too can in many ways been seen in this light. The rebels of the movement created an exciting and lively campaign but in general they failed to convert that into messages or actions for long term change. They lacked viable change agents. This latter example shows us that the momentum for change must be at least equal to the power, or arrogance, of the incumbency to resist that change.

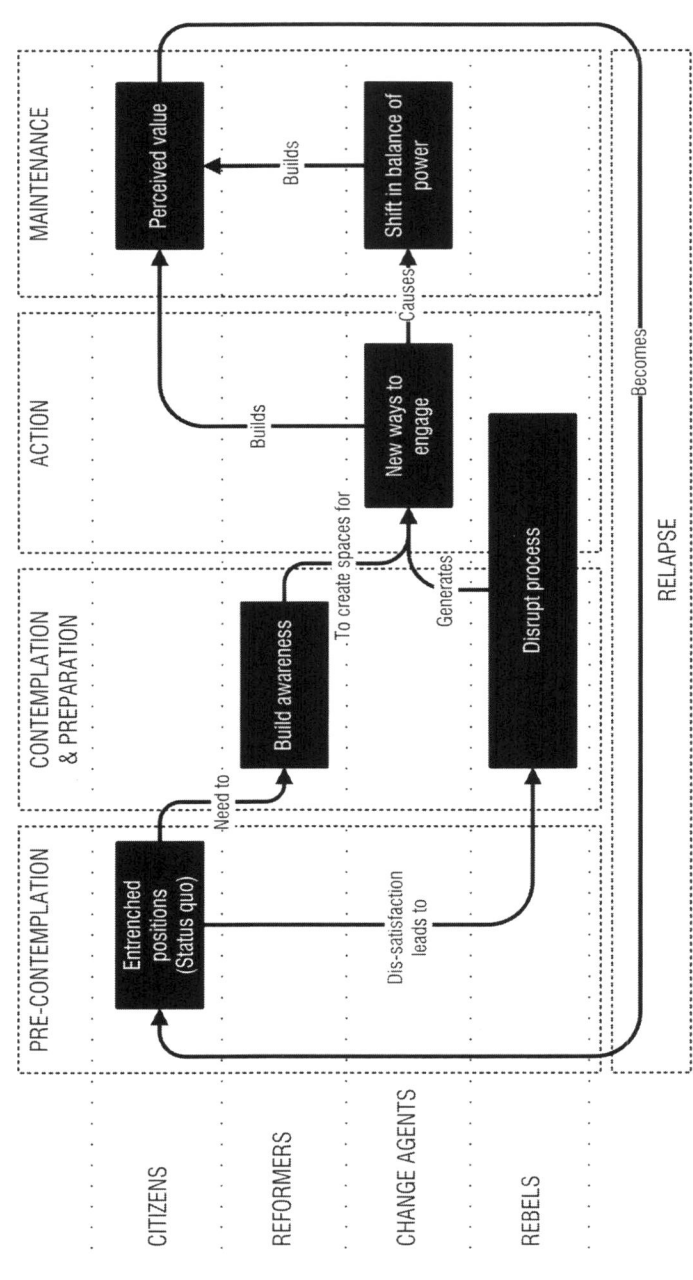

A Framework for Transformation

Or, looking at the key stages:

ENTRENCHED POSITIONS	At the start of the process the *status quo* creates a sufficient level of disaffection that early-adopters of active democracy become active in attempting to force debate and promote alternatives.
BUILDING AWARENESS	This early activity creates limited but growing awareness and activism continues. However, this group is now joined by those who see opportunities for reforming the processes.
DISRUPTION TO EXISTING PROCESSES	Identification of an opportunity has occurred and awareness-building will eventually lead to the emergence of new models of engagement. Some of these occur through the reformation of existing processes and others emerge from a transformative model that subverts existing practices. At this stage, success is dependent on key actors adopting and promoting new ways of engaging such that they can be translated into language understood by ordinary citizens.
NEW WAYS TO ENGAGE	If the change-agents have been successful, the ideas that have been promoted now start to be adopted by the mainstream and become normative practice.
SHIFT IN BALANCE OF POWER	If process has been sufficiently transformative then shifts in the balance of power should occur. Citizens have become more empowered and are more able to influence democratic process.
PERCEIVED VALUE	Models have been developed and processes refined and communicated such that citizens now see value in working this way and generally accept active democracy. At this point, active democracy becomes the status quo way of functioning.

Having reached the point where this is a general uptake of active democracy amongst citizens, new power-blocks and alliances can once again start to exert influence and the novelty of the new wears off.

Relapse is now a potential problem, where the new systems become entrenched and fail to respond to individual needs. At this point there is a risk that a new power-elite will emerge to replace the previous one. The one-time rebels have become the incumbents, the powerful, and hence the problem for a new set of rebels!

They key to avoiding relapse is to be constantly aware, continuously innovating and experiment and actively listening, sharing and co-creating. Do this and rather than risk relapsing into complacency you can energise a cycle of re-invention and continuous improvement.

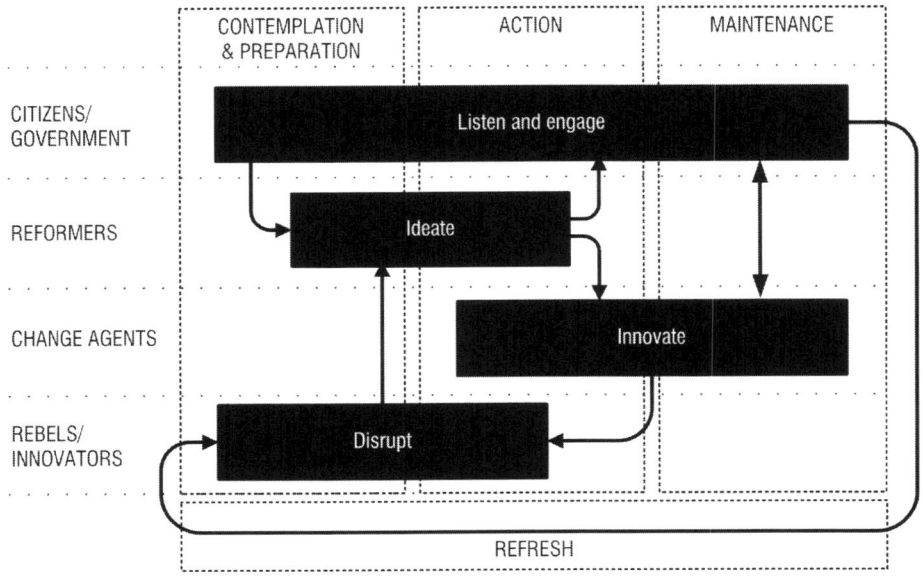

- ❖ You need to understand what stage you (and your organisation) are at.
- ❖ All of these roles are needed but they don't all work all the time.
- ❖ It's important to understand when the project will only grow by evolving to the next stage.
- ❖ Different stages need different people: initiators and innovators might not be the best project managers or the ones to operationalise.

Grounded Leadership

How do we bring all of this change together so that, instead of conflict, stalemate and frustration we have shared vision, growing trust and governments 'doing with' us? There's a lot of talk of 'us' and 'them' and this points to a fundamental problem in reconstructing democracy: how can we re-build trust and build new ways of being together if we frame key people as our 'opposition'. The answer is, of course, that we can't and so politics and democracy become adversarial, falling into the old-world ways of power and control. And this puts people off.

Fortunately there's a simple way to start to resolve these old power struggles and to establish trust in a shared process. What we've found is that there's a key role that helps active democracy work, that of intermediary or mediator. It's what we call 'grounded leadership'. A grounded leader needs to be:

- able to work effectively at a community level;
- grounded in the stakeholder community in order to be able to encourage and engage people;
- familiar with the systems and processes, protocols and informal ways of working; and
- capable of being an effective and trusted bridge linking different (and often disparate) citizens and stakeholders.

Grounded leaders are often seen as the opinion formers. They are members of the ecosystem in which they exert influence but are transparent in their role as facilitator and enabler (in other words, they are in it for the greater good not for personal power). They are often the early adopters in the life cycle of change. Establishing this position can be harder than it sounds, of course, and gaining trust across a range of stakeholders can take time and patience but often comes because grounded leaders are also seen as agents of change. They are able to drive change forward and can act as facilitators. Of course, influence might only be exercised across a limited portion of the community (especially in the early stages) but it is still possible for others to accept these individuals as capable of bridging the divides (and hopefully leading a process that closes them). So the role of 'grounded leadership' looks like this:

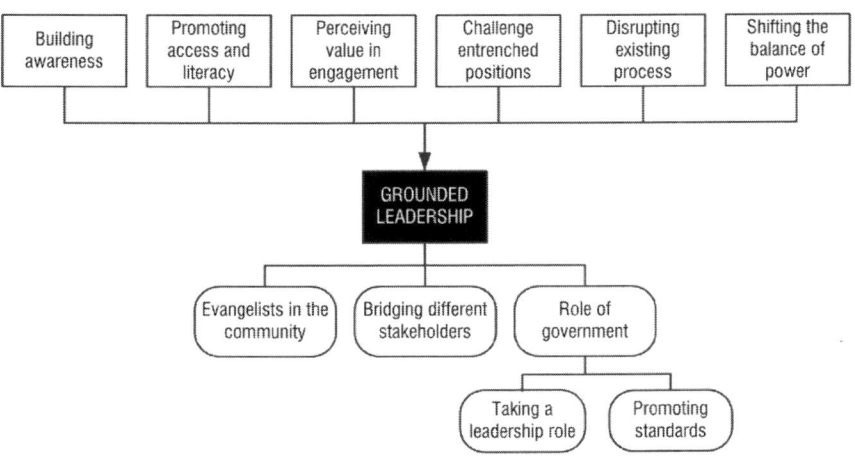

And to be one you need to have four significant attributes:

1. You're an evangelist in (and for) the community.
2. You are a trusted advocate within government.
3. You can bridge the needs and aspirations of different stakeholders.
4. You're promoting shared ways of engaging (common standards).

The role of grounded leadership emerged in our work as being critical to the establishment and success of active democracy. It's clear to us that it's not sufficient that change (or demand for change) occurs only in the community, or only in government for that matter. There has to be a willingness to do things differently on all sides and a willingness to try things out. But history, power and politics all get in the way. Grounded leaders help us to resolve this because they can speak both languages (citizen and government), understand both sides and they can mediate. They can act as neutral observers and referees (accepting that no one is ever completely neutral!), especially if they can lead the process with courage, passion and commitment.

Effective grounded leadership can share ideas and experiences across diverse groups, pull people together and they can start from a position of trust (or at least from a neutral position). So long as they are an accepted choice by all parties. Be careful if the mediators of the process are imposed as this risks aligning them with the agency imposing them; they might need to prove their independence.

To be able to motivate, engage and lead both sides – community and government – and to work together to bridge the needs of different stakeholder groups effectively trust is vital. Transparency is also critical to this process, along with setting realistic objectives, preferably ones that have been co-designed.

❖ Spread the love, bring people together and work with all sides.
❖ Need to be accepted by the community but understand the formal process too.
❖ Effective grounded leadership is a role-model for partnership.
❖ Become a disruptor, challenging the assumptions and status quo, encouraging innovation.

New Public Spaces

Policy, and therefore law, "is made by a small coterie of supporters."[59] Government policy is written by those who show up. Unfortunately, most of us don't. Most don't see the point: we don't trust government. Or politicians. And we don't believe that there's anything we can do to influence them. Digital can help change this, not set democracy on fire, suddenly re-igniting our latent passions for civic engagement. But just maybe it can break down the barriers enough so it's easier to take part. Our personal tipping point is reached sooner, sustained for longer.

None of this is new. The democratic drift in mature democracies started in the 1950s and has caused serious erosion in political participation and trust. And a concomitant complacent absolution of responsibility for our civic spaces. We delegate to elected representatives, public officials and – increasingly – private corporations.

There are significant, multi-layered barriers to democratic access for many people. Real-world problems include lack of time, money, knowledge and access. Digital exclusion creates another sub-class of citizens. They can't use new engagement platforms and are increasingly frozen-out of others. Information and political literacy

---

[59] The Power Inquiry. (2006). Power to the people. York: Joseph Rowntree Charitable Trust & Joseph Rowntree Reform Trust.

are vital pre-requisites for participation but are often poorly taught or missing altogether.

We have to ensure that new engagement methods do not further disadvantage those who are already marginalised and excluded. Without alternative methods and appropriate citizen knowledge and education, engagement risks becoming another channel for the usual suspects, a digitally savvy sub-set of the existing political class.

If we're to arrest this decline we have to make it easier to take part. We have to transform our civic spaces so that they look like the world the majority of us live in (or want to live in) – more open, social, interconnected, even games-based. Driven by issues not ideology. A lot of this can happen online but governments are not Facebook and Facebook is not government. Should we rely on unaccountable, unelected corporations to be the conduits of our 21st century democracy?

Let's bring democracy back to the public, not only through their browsers but increasingly through their smartphones. And much, much more. New public spaces need to be designed to include points for democratic participation within them. Parks, schools, libraries, even shopping malls matter – in fact it turns out the civic amenity that most of us use is the supermarket. Let's include everything from the simple, analogue and off-line places to congregate (and, yes, demonstrate – a legitimate and valuable part of our democratic heritage), through to integrated digital furniture and the legislation needed to enshrine our rights to use it.

Kiosks let those who are offline connect, contribute and learn about democracy, their local communities and beyond. Public video displays link to real-time consultations and we can harness the ever more powerful location aware devices of people nearby.

Let's make the places we live two-way, conversational. Listening as much as talking.

All of this costs money. But perhaps not as much you might imagine and the beauty of the solution lies in the communities we already have. More and more of us can bring our own tools – a smartphone and a reasoned opinion. Many cities host active developers and democratic evangelists in 'hack-days'. Using open source software, open data and community-government partnerships for co-design we can, now more than ever, bring democracy back to our public spaces and reconnect citizens with those who they elect to govern.

- ❖ Let's get democracy out of the council chamber and take it out on to the streets.
- ❖ Spread not just the message but the opportunity to make sure no one is excluded.
- ❖ Plug democracy into the places people go, public spaces and commercial spaces too.
- ❖ Think about interactivity and multi-channel, like electronic billboards and mobile.
- ❖ Get people involved in 'hacking' their future.

The Evolution of Digital Engagement

As our democratic and cultural landscapes have changed, the range of tools now available to governments and citizens has grown significantly over the last fifteen years. Engagement can now occur in many different ways and any number of different stages in the policy process. This offers the potential to engage and retain citizen participation throughout the lifecycle of policy development, service implementation and review. When we look back over the (actually quite long) history of the civic internet, we can see that there are three distinct evolutionary phases, or ages, of digital engagement.

The first age started with discussion boards. Mostly these were community based and led, governments rarely if ever got directly involved. They were useful for co-ordinating and sharing, for raising public consciousness around an issue but little else. Government agencies at this time rarely undertook any direct digital engagement and the internet was limited to publishing documents (often as large and inaccessible PDFs).

This early model of digital democracy moved into government-owned and managed platforms for engagement and consultations. These sites were usually bespoke and localised and include such things as e-Petitions. The rise in this model of digital democracy parallels the rise in digital government (or e-government). However, where the digitisation of transactional services offers clear economic benefits and process improvements, the democratic benefits are less obvious and often more intangible, leading to a more piecemeal and inconsistent uptake.

The second age of digital democracy has been overtaken and enhanced by two key factors. First is the advent of social media and second is the increasing trend towards the publication of open data repositories. In this model, citizens, government and third party agents can create 'mash-ups' and dynamic digital resources for communities to become more active citizens, linking these directly to government processes.

Open data has the benefit of increasing the transparency of government, providing better opportunities for public scrutiny of government transactions and outcomes. However, it is only effective if civic actors have the skills to analyse and manage the data. Data for data's sake is not a panacea. Both open data and engagement through social media suffer from the primary restriction of earlier phases of digital engagement, namely ownership and control.

The range and quantity of digital tools has blossomed, offering many new ways to bring together government and the public for the purposes of information, engagement and participation. Some are more effective than others and will be appropriate for different stages of the policy or legislative cycle and unhelpful for others. It is, therefore, important that, before selecting a tool, the purpose and nature of the engagement process is clearly understood. To assist with this, it is possible to group digital engagement tools into four broad categories:

DISCOVER	Research and information gathering, using available digital and off-line sources to frame an issue and to scope problem statements.
DISCUSS	Using a continuum of on- and off-line tools, source input to the problem statement and frame responses, actions and alternatives. This phase has three critical sub-components; Listen, Ask, Respond. This phase ranges from the passive to the active, including monitoring and sentiment analysis of social media as well as running interactive dialogues.
DECIDE	Participatory tools allow stakeholders to make open, transparent decisions based on the evidence available. This can include tools for polling through to deliberate fora.
DELIVER	Providing open data and the co-creation of relevant and useful interfaces into this data, new applications, campaigns and service design and delivery that result from the engagement cycle. Tools, data and applications created or exposed during this phase feedback into future discovery cycles.

The UK-based 'Digital Engagement Cookbook'[60] identifies 67 different sub-categories of digital engagement tool, which can be mapped into the categories above (this website uses slightly different descriptors but they are inherently similar):

DISCOVER	DISCUSS	DECIDE	DELIVER
Augmented Reality	Blogging	Comparators	Commodity Exchange
Content Hosting	Collaborative Editing	Crowdcasting	Data Harvesting
Debate or argument visualisation	Digital back channel	Direct Democracy	eActivism
Digital Dashboards	eClinics	Electronic Citizen Jury	Effort Distributors

---

[60] See: www.digitalengagment.org

Electronic Poll	Electronic Mailing List	eMarketplace	End user database
Enhanced Translucence	Instant Messaging	ePanels	File Sharing
eSatisfaction	Media Streaming	eParticipatory Budgeting	Group Discounting
Experience Sharing	Networking by place	ePetitions	Informed Investment Networks
Idea Sourcing	Online Chat	Interactive Surface	Interactive Voice Response (IVR)
Online Memo	Online Forums	Interactive TV	Live Co-Creation
Online Quizzes	Social Networking	Online Consultation	Online Pledges
Opinion Sourcing	Status Updates	Online Prediction Markets	Positive Influence
Rating systems	Video Views	Online Survey	Proximity Networking
Resource Sharing	Virtual Meetings	Open Contest	Social Alerting
Serious Games	Webinar	Ranking	Social Reporting
Simulations		Recommendation Systems	Software as a service
Virtual Environments		Scheduling	Time Banking
		Spatially Enhanced Consultation	

It is also important at this stage to consider not simply the tool itself but the implications of using that tool. The selection that you make is going to be further influenced by the cost and the resource implications, as the table below shows:[61]

---

[61] Miller, L. & A. Williamson (2008). Digital Dialogues Third Phase Report. London, Hansard Society/Ministry of Justice.

A Framework for Transformation

TOOL	RESOURCING IMPLICATIONS			
	PLATFORM COST	CONTENT PRODUCTION	RESPONSE TIME	INTER-ACTIVITY
Blog	Low	High	High	Medium
Forum	Low	Medium	High	High
Online chat	Low	Low	Medium	Medium
Social Networking	Low	High	Medium	High
Wikis & Structured Iterative Platforms	Low	Medium	Low	Low
e-Petitions & Polls	Medium	Low	Medium	High
Budget/Policy Simulators & Games	Medium	High	Low	High

❖ Digital is no 'one size fits all', it's important to choose the right tools for the job.

❖ The old internet was a publishing tool, the new internet is a conversation.

❖ Make sure your process is transparent and that you follow it.

❖ Involve people and keep them connected (so they become your weak ties!)

Opening up our Data

Open data has taken on a prominent focus within the digital government agenda and rightly so. Though it's just one aspect of digitising our democracy, data is[62] a vital engine to drive better decision making and to level the playing field for citizens. Open public data actively supports active democracy.

There are many reasons why governments are moving towards transparency and adopting open government principles and many more reasons why we, as citizens, should demand that our data be open by default. Whilst the G8 governments have already committed to exactly this (subject to legal restrictions, such as national security), implementation lags well behind intent.[63] When we work with governments and legislators in Latin America, for example, they see the benefits of a more transparent governance system. Being open reduces opportunities for corruption and nepotism. In Europe the motives are slightly less clear, you most often get a vaguely stated philosophical belief in transparency as being a core tenet of democracy. As we've seen in the momentum of the Open Government Partnership (OGP),[64] core parts of the public service efficiency and transparency agendas have come sharply into focus over the last two

---

[62] Yes, we know 'data' is plural but this isn't a lesson in Latin grammar: www.theguardian.com/news/datablog/2010/jul/16/data-plural-singular

[63] www.gov.uk/government/publications/open-data-charter/g8-open-data-charter-and-technical-annex; Chan, J. (2014). Policy Deep Dive: Local open data policy in Canada. Washington DC: Sunlight Foundation: sunlightfoundation.com/blog/2014/07/11/policy-deep-dive-local-open-data-policy-in-canada

[64] See: www.opengovpartnership.org

years or so. Whilst many of these (and the OGP itself) contain a commitment to partnerships with civil society, it's hard to be anything other than a little sceptical at some of the promises made compared to the realities of the process.

'Open data' in an active democracy context is about providing access to public data sets to help us hold government to account, get more involved in the decision making process and so that citizens can better understand how the public sector works (both in a macro sense or in a very real life, local sense). It allows us to audit what our parliamentarians and councillors are spending their time and our money on and it helps us to catch the bus on time. It allows all of us (government, NGOs and citizens) to 'mash up', or connect, datasets. To link what sometimes appears to be disparate datasets that can help us see things in different ways (think about the correlation between levels of street crime and incidences of street light failure or weather data, for example).

Open data is a powerful and largely positive force but there are some key questions about its cost, value and implications for society too. From an active democracy perspective, we see openness and open data as a pre-requisites. But we need to understand that, as well as the benefits, there are risks and challenges. So we want to frame some key questions that need to be answered if we are to address open data so that it benefits the whole of society. If it is to escape from the technocratic, technological or scientific arguments that it all too often risks being captured as. After all, data is our lives made digital: connected, shared, represented, aggregated. Used and mis-used. Data is a much art as science, as much narrative as algorithm. Its use is as much sociological as it is mathematical.

When we talk about 'open data' we acknowledge that the definitions we're going to use will of course remain contestable. For us then, open data is "is free to use, reuse, and redistribute".[65] Taking this a bit further, the Open Data Institute (ODI) sets out four principles that make open data effective (and, by implication, legitimate):

- [it] can be linked to, so that it can be easily shared and talked about;
- is available in a standard, structured format, so that it can be easily processed;
- has guaranteed availability and consistency over time, so that others can rely on it; and
- is traceable right back to where it originates, so others can work out whether to trust it.[66]

In other words, to be considered 'open' data has to be:

- Authentic
- Available
- Accessible
- Reusable
- Redistributable

It really only makes sense to see open data as an enabler. Its value lies indirectly in its application, not in the data itself. The digital revolution has given us not only open data but the architecture and the applications by which we can give it purpose and value. Though there remain significant challenges in terms of ensuring that the architecture itself remains open, supporting free and equitable use.

Open data offers us numerous potential benefits and so it's unsurprising that the amount of public open data in the UK more than tripled in the two years to mid-2013, with over 9,500 datasets in the

---

[65] See: opendefinition.org
[66] See: theodi.org/guide/what-open-data

public domain.[67] Sweden and the UK, like many countries, offer 'data' repositories and catalogues to make it easy to find and get at public data. New Zealand goes further and lets you request new data sets and the public can vote on which one is a priority. Licensing has of course been a thorny issue in the past as governments clung helplessly to outmoded ideas of copyright but thankfully this is largely being resolved through more appropriate methods. The UK Open Government Licence (OGL) is a subset of Crown copyright/Crown database regulation, designed to promote the use and re-use of public data sources. However, OGL makes no assumption that data is provided free to the end user and allows for both commercial and non-commercial distribution and re-use models,[68] including direct charging for access to datasets (such as the Land Registry's property price data sets[69]). OGL and other licensing systems shouldn't be confused as synonyms for 'open data'.

Why open data matters lies in its benefits. Often reported as economic, there are clear democratic benefits too and these are why opening up public data is a core tenet of active democracies.

Open data provides accountability. As a subset of the wider philosophy of public transparency (and, conversely, the publics' right to information) there is an increasing assumption, matched by the increasing availability of technology that makes it easy, that governments will share information and can now be held to account. Where secrecy breeds corruption and nepotism, transparency increases accountability, improves fairness and improves democratic outcomes. The key issue here is one of trust: transparency and trust

---

[67] See: data.gov.uk
[68] See: www.nationalarchives.gov.uk/information-management/government-licensing/about-the-ogl.htm
[69] See: www.landregistry.gov.uk/market-trend-data/public-data/price-paid-data

A Framework for Transformation

are "intrinsically linked".[70] Unfortunately, as we've already heard, fewer and fewer of us trust our governments: in the UK 90% of us believe that government is acting in the interests of a small elite.[71] Better access to better quality information can support the re-building of public trust in democratic processes.[72]

At the social level, open data increases public choice. The UK Government's Open Public Services White Paper describes how citizens can take control of their lives through direct payments, personal budgets, entitlements or choice. Open data can be used to provide comparative information and enables meaningful choice in public services. One example of this is the comparative analysis of service quality.

The government sees open data as a driver of efficiency.[73] Indeed, the inverse, that poor data leads to poor decisions, seems patently obvious. Taking this further, the provision of high quality data can be used to improve quality and outcomes in the public sector. Of course, this does not require data to be open per se but providing open data creates new opportunities for wider and more independent analysis. And open data can support wider public debate and effective user engagement, leading to better input into policy and improved service design. Consider the benefits of open data to communities and citizens, who can now be more informed when engaging with government.

---

[70] Cabinet Office (2013). Open Data White Paper: Unleashing the potential. London: HM Government. p.31.

[71] Transparency International (2013). Global Corruption Barometer 2013. www.transparency.org.uk/news-room/blog/12-blog/679-global-corruption-barometer-2013; Hansard Society (2013). Audit of political Engagement. London: Hansard Society.

[72] Williamson, A. (2011). Disruption and empowerment: Embedding citizens at the heart of democracy. Journal of eDemocracy and Open Government. www.jedem.org/article/view/52

[73] Cabinet Office (2010). Efficiency review by Sir Philip Green. London: HM Government.

Open data offers economic potential. Opening public data sets allows technology developers to add value by developing software and applications for specific needs, examples of this include mapping data and live transport data from organisations like Transport for London, now available to commuters through a myriad of smartphone apps (not all of which are free to use). The app market highlights an inconsistency (and perhaps the immaturity) of the open data 'market', whereby commercial developers can create a revenue-generating product from freely available public data with no requirement to share this revenue with the originator of the data. Should commercial users pay a licence fee or enter into a revenue-share arrangement thereby supporting the cost of opening data?

But, like most things digital, it's not a panacea. Whilst supportive of open data, the Open Rights Group sees three risks.[74] First is that the protection of vested interests (and this could potentially include revenue streams) can "derail plans to open up government data" as can poor governance, cultural stagnation and lack of process and standards (such as meta-data).[75] Second is that, as the use of open data becomes more commonplace, we are moving from its simple use by citizens to the use of data for complex decision making and that this area is less well understood. Thirdly, they note the risks to privacy.[76]

The Guardian raises the additional risk of the 'feedback effect' of open data. They suggest "that the very act of publishing the data will influence the quality of future data" and this in turn highlights the problem of accessing, interpreting and using open data: does data suggesting a school or hospital is performing poorly lead to a vicious cycle of abandonment and further decline? Analysing datasets

---

[74] Hand, D. (2013, 10-Jul-2012). Open data is a force for good, but not without risks. www.guardian.co.uk/society/2012/jul/10/open-data-force-for-good-risks

[75] Martin, S., Foulonneau, M., Turki, S., Ihadjadene, M. (2013). Open data: Barriers, risks and opportunities. ECEG 2013, Como, Italy.

[76] See: www.openrightsgroup.org/campaigns/opendata

(particularly complex and linked datasets) requires considerable expertise and the risks associated with incorrect, inaccurate and misleading analyses are significant (we talked about the inability of some government departments to accurately use data earlier).

This brings us to the issue of public awareness and the wider understanding of open data. A recent report from Sciencewise describes public understanding as "generally low". Open data is seen as "an abstract issue with unclear benefits to everyday life" and that there "may also be a lack of clarity for members of the public over exactly what is meant by 'open data'". In particular the public appears to struggle with the concepts of private and public data.[77] And privacy issues (perceived or real) lie at the heart of concerns for many people over open and linked data. So much so that it is clearly articulated in government policies that all open data must be anonymised (whether this is through aggregation or anonymisation). O'Hara recommends that privacy needs must be addressed through the development of good practice, including pre-release evaluation of data sets and the creation of transparency panels, that the technical as well as legal aspects of privacy (which currently dominate the discourse) must be addressed and that, where data has privacy implications appropriate controls must be considered.[78]

We'd also like to highlight that there needs to be a wider conversation about where our data lives. Does our personal data exist in a range of public databases or do I own it and keep it in my own data repository? Who can control it, ensure its veracity and pro-actively allow others, such as government agencies, to use it?

---

[77] Sciencewise (2013). Public views on open data. London: Sciencewise.
[78] O'Hara, K. (2012).Transparent government, not transparent citizens: A report on privacy and transparency for the Cabinet. www.gov.uk/government/uploads/system/uploads/attachment_data/ file/61279/transparency-and-privacy-review-annex-a.pdf.

It's certainly not good enough for governments to simply release open data in a laissez-faire manner. The 2012 Open Data White Paper makes it clear that government has a co-creation role in ensuring that the right data is released, in the right formats.[79] Because governments cannot predict "with any degree of certainty how data is being used in all cases or how it is stimulating growth and innovation" it is important to develop a "clear engagement strategy with those third parties that are often our primary data users". It's important to work collaboratively with these primary users of open datasets to improve the viability and value of open data.

We believe that there's undeniable potential for open data to support the transformation of the publics' relationship with government. Open data is a key asset on the road to active democracies because openness, and the data it delivers, fundamentally underpin the transparency and accountability of our democratic institutions. Yet the emergent nature of the 'open data' sector, creates challenges over what is and is not 'open' and resistance to releasing data sets – particularly from the public when the release hints at exposing personal information, such as in the UK government's proposals to release tax and health data.

This starkly highlights the very real risks to privacy and lack of public awareness as well as the requirement for new skills if we are to maximise the democratic benefits. And it leads us to pose six questions that need to be addressed if we are to have a mature and rational debate over the pros and cons of open data and its strategically important place in an active democracy:

1. What are the policy and democratic implications of open data: Better decisions and lower service costs versus manipulation, misinformation and information overload?

---

[79] Cabinet Office (2013). Open Data White Paper: Unleashing the potential. London: HM Government

2. How are our concepts of privacy to evolve and be protected in the age of open data?
3. How is the public to be engaged and educated so they can understand the benefits and the risks of open data?
4. How are we to overcome the deficit in information literacy that open data risks not simply perpetuating but widening?
5. Should 'open data' always be free at point of use or can we accept a blend of guaranteed 'civic access' and revenue sharing commercial licensing that can help underwrite the costs of data provision?
6. How do we develop effective protocols for managing the open release of public data (do we need to consider how transparent the transparency process itself is)?

❖ Public data should be open by default.

❖ Data is our life made digital so it must represent our narrative as well as our statistics.

❖ 'Open' is a contestable term and we need to resolve when public data is free and open.

❖ Openness brings concerns for privacy that we must take seriously and we must resolve issues of control over personal data and digital architectures to ensure openness, transparency and veracity.

❖ We have to address the lack of public understanding of both the purpose and value of open data.

❖ Open data is of enormous value to citizens and communities but to harness it we need people who can understand it and use the tools.

We Need to Transform Organisations Too

Organisations are made up of people. People, who in their everyday life, make decisions based on inputs and experiences. Civil servants have an enormous power to direct, control and change an organisation's focus and processes. They are led by political, elected officials who bring forward policies aiming to realise societal change and transform communities. Leadership in government comes from both sides. Leaders come in a variety of shapes and forms in organisations, with varying abilities and skills. However we choose to look at the challenges of transformation in general and towards active democracy specifically, there is also the need to address the challenge of leadership.

Democratic transformation starts with us. Organisational transformation starts when this personal transformation starts to occur within its leaders. Management experts like Richard Barrett[80], Otto Scharmer[81] and Peter Senge[82] all tell us that you cannot transform an organisation without the explicit personal transformation of the key individuals who lead it. Is this really true?

---

[80] Barrett, R. (2014). The Values-Driven Organization: Unleashing Human Potential for Performance and Profit. London: Routledge

[81] Scharmer, O. & Kaeufer, K. (2013). Leading from the emerging future. San Francisco: Berrett-Koehler

[82] Senge, P. (2006). The Fifth Discipline: The art and practice of the learning organization (2nd Ed). London: Random House

It is perhaps a continuum but, as we see it, it is definitely a requisite for change and transformation. Leadership is more about a relationship than a formal position or title. Being a leader is being a role model. You must become someone whose actions are mimicked and repeated throughout an organisation. So, yes, organisational transformation starts with the personal transformation of the leaders. And leader's actions are contagious. So if organisations need to transform, leaders have to transform too. Moving to intimacy and co-creation requires dedicated work in several dimensions and an attitude of active learning rather than assumed knowing.

To get started we need a better map. The map we often use this map to help us decide upon strategies of transformation:

This tells us that transformation cannot happen in isolation. That transformation has to be interlinked and intertwined to become effective. The map needs to show us where we are right now and where we have to go. It needs to show us the hidden assets and visual structures that are enabling, could enable or are preventing the new behaviours we desire to emerge and evolve. As strategy, structure and culture are interlaced. They need to be developed simultaneously in order to reach the vision and create value for stakeholders.

Let's briefly sketch out an organisational transformation strategy where the *vision* is one of realising active democracies. Better democracy expressed thorough the principles of trust and resilience and the ability to meet the complex challenges through co-creative and constructive principles are the desired *value*. This is both what the organisation wants to bring about for itself and enable to emerge in society. As public-sector organisations will be a vital component in this transformation it is valid to ask about their *ability* to deliver and transform. Is there any sense of urgency and opportunity? Is there a basic trust? What of the ability for leaders and co-workers in democratic structures to transform? What does the *theory of change* look like in action? Remember your theory of change is just that, a theory. You have to connect it to a call to action to give it real life, theory will not change democracy, only actions do.

What does a *strategy* that democratic leaders have co-designed to steadily direct and facilitate towards the vision look like? We need to consider the enabling structures, what is in place and what needs to be designed, re-designed and engrained in the organisational culture of everyday work? Indeed, is there a supporting and enabling *culture* to enable the desired *strategy* to emerge towards the *vision*? Is the coherence between values and culture enabling organisational energy and the everyday positive behaviour of leaders and co-workers? This simple example of questions and their inter-linkages can be used to sketch out the outline of an organisations transformation towards active democracies.

❖ Organisations can only change when people do!

❖ Use the map to co-create and realise a holistic strategy that accepts the multiple dimensions necessary to work with.

❖ Accept that transformation is an endurance race, a demanding process that requires patience.

❖ Look for coherence between your actions and your values.

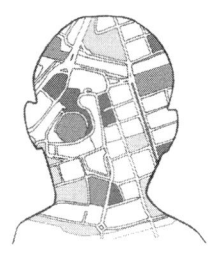

Road Map for Active Democracies

From Engagement to Action

We have to move beyond the theoretical, beyond the conversations about transforming democracy and, at some point, take real and tangible actions that can lead to change. This is hard. It's hard if you're on the outside and you feel excluded, minimised and ignored. It's hard if you work in the system and, though you sense the wave of change that's needed, you have no idea where to start. First of all, let's recognise that active democracies don't waste energy on oppositional conflict, we're all in this for the same reason – to transform the system so democracy works better for all of us. In this book we've painted a picture that shows how we need people from each side – citizens, officials and politicians – in order to build the future together. Conversation and dialogue is the fuel, grounded leadership gets us doing things together and technology supports this by being a connector, distributor and aggregator. But it's always going to be people that really matter.

Active democracy is a process that starts with disruption. The level of change required demands that we disrupt the way things are and start with innovation. That doesn't mean throw everything we have away, but it does mean question and challenge it. All of this takes courage and courage requires heart and passion. It also takes personal power but in an active democracy this power is directed towards the common good and is not used for personal benefit. It needs us to bring people along with us and, as grounded leaders, we can connect but ultimately others will only join if we demonstrate the principles of active democracy in our own actions. As Maya Angelou said:

One isn't necessarily born with courage, but one is born with potential. Without courage, we cannot practice any other virtue with consistency. We can't be kind, true, merciful, generous, or honest.[83]

We talked about these at the start of the book:

- Control is over-rated;
- Power used to create personal advantage will always fail;
- Crowds are better at creating the future; and
- Reflect on the impact of your actions on trust-building.

What this boils down to is openness; being open to connect, transparent about the aims and the process, sharing data, conversations and ideas. Establish networks and allow trust to build through our actions. These can be internal, in a community or beyond. This is what a group of local government officers told us they needed to make their democracy more active:

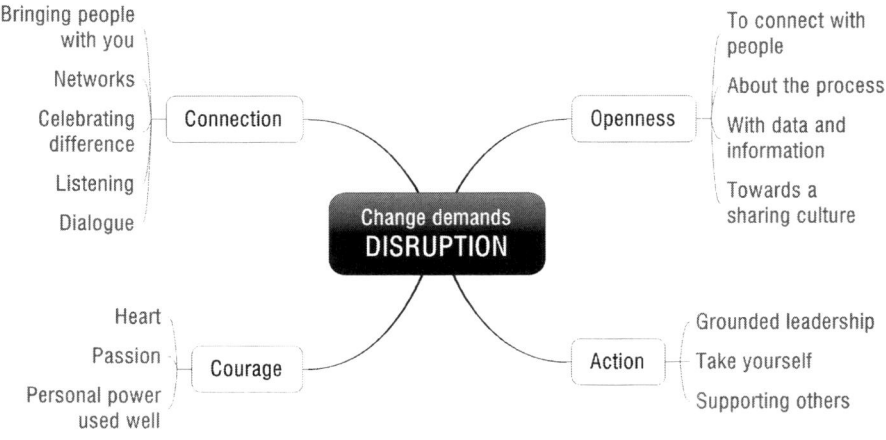

[83] Maya Angelou in an interview with USA Today, March 5, 1988.

How do we do this? What are the triggers and the cues that we can establish to build authentic relationships and establish active democracies? These will, of course, vary for every place, organisation, region and country. There's no one size fits all! So, it's important to think about and talk about the internal triggers that will compel people to take action:

- Who are they?
- What brought them here?
- Where do they want to be?

We've got to generate calls to action that engage people and then hold, contain and retain them through building positive democratic habits. Many of us are at best casual participants in our democracy, we don't have established patterns for co-creation, participation or action. Fortunately, we can build on the weak ties (particularly driven by digital media) to increase the 'stickiness'. If we want to get people up and active, involved in deciding their own futures, we need to help them establish democracy-positive habits and then they need to go and help others too. Let's consider:

- What are the habits you need to build or re-enforce for your active democracy?
- Where and when do these occur?
- What value do they generate (for the community as well as the individual)?
- What are the vitamins (nice to haves) and the painkillers (need to haves)?

How can you bring people together to discuss, debate and ultimately co-design solutions to the problems people are facing, the problems they are trying to solve. How can you connect them up with others who share their experiences, frustrations and desires or who have the skills they lack? When you're designing your own active democracy, your own innovation process or campaign, start to explore and understand the following five factors:

- How long will it take?
- How much will it cost?
- Who needs to be involved?
- What effort will be needed?
- How does this follow or challenge the accepted norms of the community?

Active democracies involve a cycle of investment in better personal and societal outcomes. Things work better the more they happen and become normative, the sooner you are able to establish a shift in perception. In the case of democracy, this is from a perception of elitism, control and disconnection to one of open, co-creating and connected – from arrogance to intimacy. Once this has started to build you need consistency and re-enforcement to build and maintain and escalate commitment and trust. And you need to avoid cognitive dissonance, do what you say, say what you do.

> ❖ Change demands disruption.
> ❖ Disruption requires courage and openness.
> ❖ We have to build new democracy-positive habits.
> ❖ Active democracies are part of a cyclical investment in better persona and societal outcomes.

Making Participation Count

We need to connect more, talk more, listen more? Yes! But how are we to do this? More importantly, how are we to do this in timely, meaningful and appropriate ways? Co-production and partnerships are great and we need them but at some point someone has to make a decision, start the process, choose a method to connect with a wider public. We have to have the courage to light the blue touch paper and wait for ignition! There are a myriad of ways we can connect our communities and build better participation in democracy but they will fail if we don't get the right people connected at the right time. We have to choose methods that overcome the challenge of always hearing the usual voices, that reach out to people who care but feel excluded. Often, we have to select tools with imperfect knowledge and in constrained surroundings. Whatever we do, let's remember that creating choice is different from letting people decide. If we're to build collaborative, networked models then we need everyone involved. Ideally, this means at the thinking and design stages, not just presenting a list of pre-agreed alternatives later in the cycle.

When we connect to people authentically we have to choose carefully, not just the tools but the timing, the place, the space and the language. Different methods obviously have different strengths and weakness, work well here but fail over there.

You can rightly expect that the methods you choose will affect the information you get and the outcomes of the process. It's helpful to think about the level of participation needed at any time. Think about this on a scale that goes from ignoring the public ('do nothing', in other words) through to where decision making is fully inclusive and participatory:[84]

- **Ignore** the public.
- **Inform** the public and other stakeholders, keeping them up to date with what is proposed and/or happening.
- **Consult** directly by going out and seeking public feedback on the proposals or input to the process.
- **Involve** the public directly in the process, ensure they are given a voice and their concerns recognised and acknowledged.
- **Collaborate** by working in partnership with the public.
- **Empower** the public by putting decision making in their hands.

Now, of course, we're going to say that we'd like you to be at the collaborative and empowering end of this continuum. But, as we said earlier on, there are times when this is neither the right approach or realistic. And what is right will change through the life cycle of a project.

It is though rather difficult to imagine a situation where 'ignore' is ever going to be the best approach! We've included it here because it is all too often the default position of arrogant governments.

We're not going to prescribe whether the engagement technique is digital, face to face or blended either. This needs to be determined by the circumstances and context, not any prevailing fashion or expediency. The pros and cons of digital engagement are explored earlier in this book too. We do want to highlight that you can use multiple techniques together or over the life of a project, you can

---

[84] Derived from the IAP2 Spectrum of Public of Participation (see: www.iap2.org)

repeat the same techniques in different places, at different times. And you can aggregate and share the results of different engagement exercises.

This chapter can't be a comprehensive guide to every possible method of public engagement.[85] We want to highlight some of the key attributes of a small range of different and popular engagement methods, to give you some idea of the variety of tools and techniques that are available. The examples we've chosen range from the traditional to the more radical, from those that work well for small-scale engagement to techniques that can be used for large groups and across whole communities. We hope this will start you thinking about what might work for you. The point we're trying to get across here is that good practice in participation is an art, not a science. Though there is plenty of scope for 'bad practice' there is no such thing as 'best practice'; circumstances and events will always vary and you need to remain flexible, vigilant and responsive.

Method	What it is	What it's good for	Typical risks
Written consultation	Traditional method, can easily be extended online and to new media.	A wide range of opinions over a longer time period.	Lacks a deliberative element; can be seen as too formal; favours the well-resourced.
Town hall meetings	Face to face (or digital online equivalent) public meetings.	Getting people together to hear a range of views.	Time and space constrained; attract usual suspects and can be dominated.
Neighbourhood forums	Face to face small group meetings, usually involving citizens, officials	Local issues and small group discussion.	Time and space constrained; attract usual suspects and can be dominated.

[85] We recommend you visit the participationcompass.org website, developed by Involve, for a wide ranging set of resources and articles on participation methods.

Method	What it is	What it's good for	Typical risks
	and representatives.		
Advisory groups	Small ongoing reference groups of experts and stakeholders.	Focussed discussion on topic.	Can be biased and seen as elitist.
Citizen panels	Juries or panels can be convened to hear evidence, deliberate and make recommendations.	Representative, deliberative and able to hear a wide range of voices.	Need strong processes and methods or risk failure.
Focus groups	Small group, focussed qualitative discussions.	Analysing specific issues.	Tend not to be representative.
Crowdsourcing	Collectively gather and evaluate (or rank) ideas online.	Draws out creative and original ideas and allows public to evaluate and prioritise.	Ideas can be dominated and voting biased by interest group campaigning.
Hackdays	Co-creative gatherings where people from a range of backgrounds actively prototype solutions.	Creative and energising spaces where innovative ideas will emerge.	Prototypes are just that, without investment in follow up hackdays rarely deliver real benefits.
Scenario planning	Intensive multi-day workshops that bring together a range of views and backgrounds with the aim of developing future scenarios.	When consensus seems impossible, scenarios can help create shared visions, so well suited to conflict situations.	An intensive process that requires significant commitment of time and energy.

Participatory budgeting	Though it can vary in focus and scale, it fundamentally involves communities coming together to allocate budgets for services.	Informed decision making, community cohesion, collaborative democracy.	Can be time consuming and resource heavy; often what is done is too light to be really participatory.

Notice we've not said anything about who organises, hosts or facilitates your participation? That's because in an active democracy it could be any one of the actors involved. Ideally it will be a partnership between citizens and government. There are times when it's appropriate and right that engagement is formal and institutionally-led. There are also times when this is counter-productive and will deliver you weak outcomes. Equally there are opportunities to open up engagement to groups that have previously felt excluded, support them to undertake these processes themselves or with support and to bring people together in new ways. Different techniques will elicit different results and will work better or worse with different groups. Actively work to ensure proper representation but remain flexible and ensure that you include aggregation of the outcomes into the process from the start.

Effective engagement does not end with an event. It's critically important that whatever is done is situated in the wider context, that it understands and acknowledges the social and cultural settings, as well as the political environment. Good facilitation is key to good outcomes. It's pointless holding a meeting simply for 10% of the audience to dominate with their well-worn extremes. Good decisions are almost always brokered in the middle of the room and 'single issue fanatics' are rarely the ones best placed to lead this.

We're completely against consultation as a 'box ticking exercise', it's pointless, patronising and it will backfire in terms of longer term disengagement. If you're going to engage, then do it properly! Be prepared to listen to uncomfortable opinions, debate and make decisions based on what you hear. Engagement cannot work in a vacuum, you have to design the processes around it to ensure that what you hear is fed back into the decision making and that participants know how, where and when this will happen. Consider too the feedback loop, how will you let people know about the decisions that are made and how will you relate those decisions back to what's just happened?

Any and every engagement exercise is an opportunity to build trust in the process, to engage people who have felt excluded or not seen value in participating. As the author Arundhati Roy said:

> We know of course there's really no such thing as the 'voiceless'. There are only the deliberately silenced, or the preferably unheard.[86]

Let people down and you will re-enforce their dislocation and mistrust. Demonstrate inclusivity, partnership and listening, prove that their words can affect your actions, and you might just start them on the road to greater involvement.

Understanding the outcome of participation and its interaction with process and the decisions made is an important part of building active democracies. We can certainly evaluate the project but perhaps we need to reflect on and evaluate the processes we use too. In an active democracy we see everything as a learning opportunity, and by this we mean active learning. This is a chance to use action research

---

[86] Roy, A. (2004, Nov 4). Peace and the new corporate liberation theology. 2004 Sydney Peace Prize Lecture: University of Sydney.

techniques to help institutions and participants to get better at participation. You can use formal methods like recruiting independent evaluators or holding focus groups. Feedback loops built into the original process design can encourage reflexive commentary, whether it's in the form of confidential feedback or by creating an open space for discussion. Participation is an active process informed by theory, so our actions and experiences can be used to drive the development of that theory, to make our future engagement better.

- ❖ Participation is an art not a science.
- ❖ Choose the method that suits the circumstances, never be driven by the tools.
- ❖ The tools you use will affect the outcome.
- ❖ Focus on inclusivity.
- ❖ Evaluate, reflect, learn and refine.
- ❖ Build in reflexivity and feedback loops.

Innovating Alongside the Organisation

Traditional organisations tend to be hierarchical and this is replicated in our democratic systems, with parallel structures for officers and members. Hierarchical. Siloed. Contained. You might say closed.

In fact, most of our democratic world looks like this:

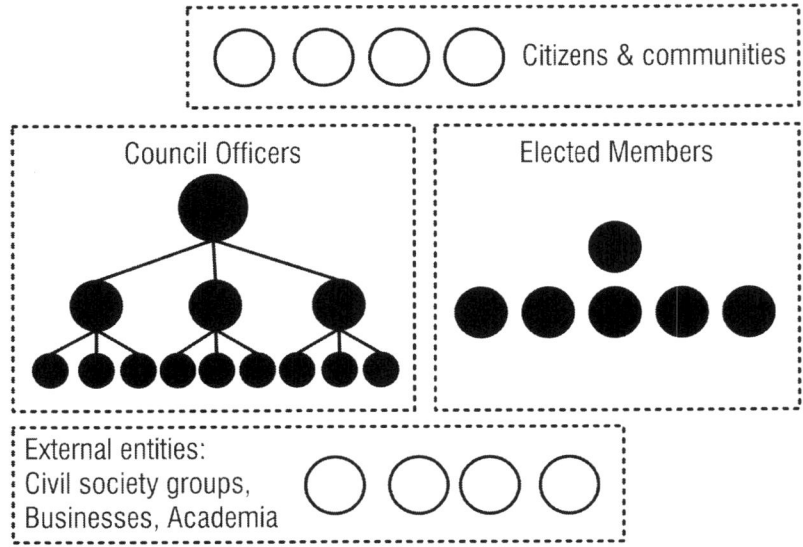

It's been fashionable to re-organise this model for a long time. We've seen various clusters and matrices appear and disappear from fashion. Generally speaking these restructures fail. Transformation usually occurs because we want to make organisations more efficient, innovative or responsive (to customers or, in the case of government, the public). But too often things simply drift back to something that resembles the original hierarchy.

So we thought about why. Let's start with a dangerous assumption, one that's all too often made, which is to assume that poor managers and bad processes are the result of the hierarchy. Turns out they're not. They are the consequence of bad management and poor process design. Which can occur anywhere.

When we break it all down, it turns out that hierarchies actually work well for what they were designed to do, that is, run an organisation. Run properly, they are operationally effective and efficient.[87] And that's the key: they do what they were designed to do. But they don't necessarily do what we need them to do now! So how do we re-shape organisations into responsive, listening and co-creative organisations without destroying what actually works? It turns out that the weak link is innovation (funny that!). What hierarchies (in this case, councils, governments, parliaments and big NGOs) are poor at is generating innovation and leading rapid change. When you understand that the hierarchy is designed to enhance operational efficiencies, this makes complete sense. Unfortunately, if you've read this far, you'll have realised by now that we believe that democracy needs innovation and the ability to change rapidly and it needs both of these urgently!

---

[87] Leavitt, H.J. (2003). Why Hierarchies Thrive. Harvard Business Review: hbr.org/2003/03/why-hierarchies-thrive/ar/1

This all comes about because the value of the hierarchy lies in its solidity. Solid objects don't easily bend. Or as John Kotter puts it "any company that has made it past the start-up stage is optimized for efficiency rather than for strategic agility".[88] And right now we need strategic agility as well as efficiency.

The modern world requires a level of pliability, particularly (and increasingly) within democratic organisations. Failure to adapt and change has led to democratic drift and a fall in public trust. We don't want to see governments wasting their time and our money transforming into some new management structure based on a fad, we want them to recognise the inherent value in the structure and focus on removing or at least mitigating the weaknesses – and making the organisation responsive and open can do this.

"So it's broke, but don't fix it" is that what you're saying? No. What we're saying is don't break it anymore. And then fix it from the inside. To start a fire, you need oxygen, heat and fuel. To innovate you need ideas, passion and action. Above all, you need a culture that can let this happen (including accepting the concomitant need to fail safely). We believe the wider democratic ecosystem is a network but we're realistic enough to recognise that some of the organisations in it will remain hierarchical, so let's accept that and look for ways to re-model the hierarchy to engage more openly with the network around it.

Google is one of the most innovative companies in history but it goes even further. 'Google X' is a radical project lab that embraces radical thinking, even so far as to see failure as "not precisely the goal at Google X. But in many respects it is the means." This is a project space that brings together a diverse group of creators, thinkers and intellectuals to solve problems. Ultimately, it can create amazing and innovative new products, such as Google's driverless car or Google

---

[88] Kotter, J. (2012). Accelerate! Harvard Business Review: hbr.org/2012/11/accelerate/ar/1

Glass. But on the way it fails. A lot. 'X' is itself an experiment in trying to re-design the way a corporate lab works. Google have done this by accepting risk as inherent right across the process and not being bound by the narrow limits of their current business.[89]

We're not suggesting you get this radical, it's perhaps one extreme end of the innovation concept. But we are highlighting some key attributes that Google understands. Specifically, the need to radically innovate away from everyday constraints, the importance of failure to ultimate success and that innovation is so often iterative. To contain these concepts we've conceived a symbiotic innovation network, formed around a physical and virtual hub. It's effectively a cross-organisational space for ideation, innovation and experimentation but the key to success is that it exists alongside and remains linked to the traditional hierarchy: it doesn't replace it.

This is a place where the internal innovators and even your external rebels (as we called them earlier) can come together. It's a space to think, experiment, prototype, fail and refine. But to work, the model needs buy-in from strategic people across your organisation and pathways back into the hierarchy to deliver change effectively. There's no need for universal support, resistance and scepticism is natural, sometimes even useful and it's better to spend the energy doing rather than defending.

This isn't a fashion statement, it's long-term re-thinking of how you make your organisation responsive and adaptable, about how you equip it for change, both physically and philosophically, and prepare it for a new world. Nor is what we're suggesting a plaything for senior managers and techies; the network has to be open to everyone with an idea and is about building dynamic open teams to design, explore and

---

[89] Gertner, J. (2014, Apr). The truth about Google X: an exclusive look behind the secretive lab's closed doors. Fast Company. Available at fastcompany.com/3028156/united-states-of-innovation/the-google-x-factor

build. This includes bringing in external people. In the case of government, this can be from NGOs, academia and individual citizens. People can be seconded on a part-time or time-limited basis but above all they need to physically gather to talk about the challenges they face, exchange ideas and work on solutions.

The model we propose is entirely hands-on and practical but that doesn't mean it is out of control. Actions, reactions and decisions still need to be collected and the innovation model will work more effectively when it's informed by evidence, and is praxis-based. There's also the need to have a good process behind everything too. Even if innovation sometimes appears to be a little chaotic, there really is a method to the perceived madness!

The challenge is to translate start-up thinking into operational reality. This is as much cultural as it is technical, so the physical innovation space needs to mirror the intellectual space – open, flexible, reconfigurable and above all visible to the wider organisation, not tucked away in a basement! Ideas can be floated, hacked and tried out. The ones that show promise are able to migrate back over to the main organisation and this is helped by the innovation hub being visible and accessible to others beyond it. The exchange process becomes one of lighting fires of innovation throughout. This is as much a part of the fuelling process for the innovation network, showing others that the network can deliver practical benefits.

Above all the innovation network has to be shaped to you, so whilst we can suggest a model, the implementation has to be unique to your needs and culture.

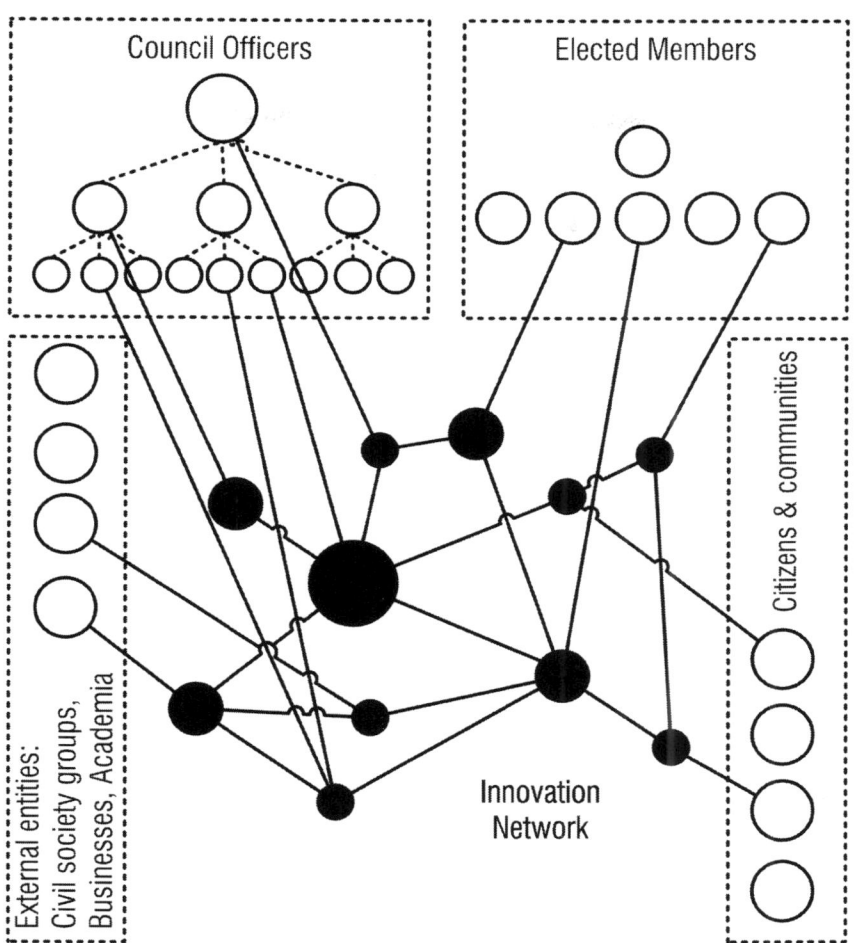

Council Officers

Elected Members

External entities:
Civil society groups,
Businesses, Academia

Citizens & communities

Innovation
Network

- ❖ Networks are better at innovation.
- ❖ Hierarchies do well at the operational details.
- ❖ To adapt the hierarchies in our democratic organisations we need to create a culture where innovation comes from anyone at any time.
- ❖ Create spaces that visible value radical ideas, soft failure and active learning.
- ❖ Make the hierarchies permeable so innovation is easily drawn back in and, in doing so, the organisation itself transforms from the inside.

Lean, Agile and Active

Resilience, complexity and learning are intertwined. Just surviving, then being able to thrive, in complex systems is a totally different skillset from the ones many of us have grown up with. It's not just that we need new skills, if we are to embrace complexity then we need a new mind-set too. Throughout this book we've argued that linear thinking is inadequate for a networked world, it's no longer the optimum way to deliver change amidst uncertainty. Your ability and effectiveness at being able to control, predict and, in advance, define all possible routes results in a leadership of arrogance and control. Increasingly, in the complex milieu that is the networked society, it leads to failure.

Co-creating might be the path less walked yet it is the one we need to practice. At the heart of complexity lies the view of non-linearity and connectedness both in people and structures. Hence our models of change and learning need to change, going from a linear to an iterative model of action with feedback loops that embed learning. We also need to re-learn, to re-understand, time, place and pace and to embrace failure as a key part of success. We believe that a symbiotic network for innovation and co-creation can support these ways of working. But doing this requires change, risk and, above all, courage. To succeed you need to choose the right methods. In a networked ecosystem, pace and frequency is better suited to small-scale prototyping and experimentation. This is how we implement the scenario planning and backcasting models we talked about earlier.

We're aiming towards a vision, a target, but it's not a straight line and requires us to constantly check and re-check that the target is still the same, in the same place and is valid. We no longer plan the project in detail, we accept that iterations will change perceptions and requirements. So we target short 'sprints', periods of action, followed by reflection and learning.

This lean process allows us to be more frugal and use less of our resources and it maximizes learning from every iteration. A looping (double) mode of action shows us early on what works and what doesn't. This kind of experimental approach requires a higher tolerance for uncertainty and risk, but the modern world is one of uncertainty and risk. Pretending otherwise is dangerously flawed. We don't have the answers when we start out, often we don't even have the right questions!

An experimental ability in our new leaders is built upon an attitude of embracing this uncertainty. Today's prevailing reflexive action of many leaders facing complexity is one of holding firm and closing down to control. This needs a mind shift so we can feel comfortable letting go and opening up. Not easy to do, especially in a situation where the expectations are piling up and the public assumes and desires certain behaviours from its leaders in terms of action and answers. Doing the opposite, opening up and inviting them in to co-create answers (and questions!) and then honouring the process is a truly courageous and conscious act. An active democracy needs courageous and conscious leaders who feel comfortable not having the answers and sharing and embracing insights of uncertainty with others in the network. And as we discussed earlier, leaders can emerge from anywhere in the ecosystem at any time, so long as you reduce the friction and the control.

We think change is important. We have to recognise that the status quo (particularly in democratic systems) is the problem, is often unsustainable and that we don't, on our own, know how to fix it. We need to embed the constant of change so it becomes habitual but recognise too that, once we do, our own innovation risks becoming stale and problematic (we've discussed this earlier when we talked about the democracy life cycle in the "Why Personal Engagement Matters"chapter). So it makes sense that we also need new ways of doing projects and making change happen, from the big to the small.

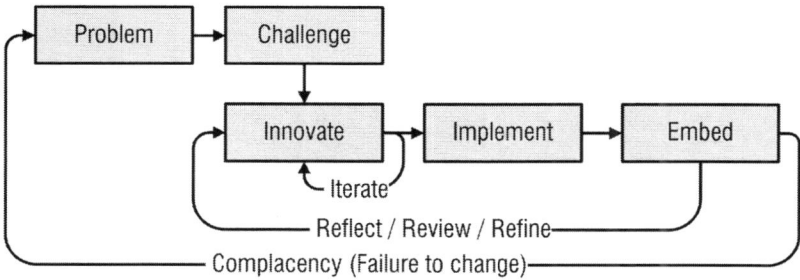

To help overcome these problems we recommend working with agile methods. Not because they are fashionable amongst internet companies but because they work. They are also not new (Andy has been working with agile methods for over 25 years), so there's a wealth of information available. We recommend this approach because it manages risk in an unclear world, is built with the user in mind and lends itself to both rapid prototyping and co-creation. This is a technique built around innovation, experimentation, failing in order to learn and learning for the future.

There are many variations on agile and lean methods and you should find the one that works best for you, we're in no way prescriptive. But based on our own experience, we'd suggest that the methods you choose cover the following lifecycle phases:

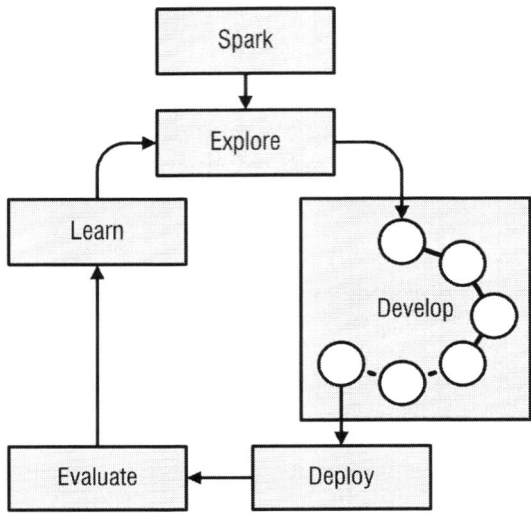

This is the whole agile project, it's also the sub components of each section. For us, agile is best seen as an almost infinitely regressive method, where the overarching project is seen as a 'sprint' made up of smaller 'sprint' components. The 'sprint' is a core concept of manageability and creative focus. Go back to the backcasting framework discussed earlier and here you have a vision but not the detail. The detail starts in a sprint and ends with you learning what happened and reviewing the goal. Now choose whether to continue or to pivot in a new direction. This is agile in action, it is also action learning and it's critical that our active democracies become learning ecosystems.

For each detailed sprint within a project, set a short time frame (hours or days), decide on an end point: know when you're done, even if right now you don't know what the answer or even the question is. Which, of course, is a challenge but this is where experience and intuition come in. Our experience tells us that you're usually finished just at the last moment before you realise it (it's that next act that tips things over and hence why aiming for perfection is fraught with failure-).

Work on the problem. Iteratively explore ideas, problems and possible solutions, be open and don't lock out views because they are contrary or poorly understood. Use prototyping to develop the ideas quickly, even in parallel streams, using lateral techniques. You don't always need to write code to demonstrate software or use real bricks to demonstrate a building concept – be creative! Once it's all done, reflect on the process and the product, reflect on what you wanted and what you now understand that you didn't before. Be honest about the gaps in your knowledge and the flaws in your product.

It's a truism in agile development that 'good enough' is in fact good enough! You aren't aiming for perfection first time, just enough to get you started. This is an iterative process and it can be improved, refined and polished through use, evaluation and reflexive learning. To start off with, aim for a minimum viable product (MVP), this is the smallest, simplest instantiation of the idea that can go forward to the users to work with, play around with and evaluate.

Don't get fixated on development and delivery either, we don't believe that this is enough for success and is an approach that creates unnecessary risk. Lean methods in general will go beyond the design and manufacturing phases to include the evaluation of what you've done and this is absolutely critical for active democracy. It's also critical that you always remember the user. Always!

We believe very strongly in using techniques such as action research that are reflexive and critical ways of understanding problems and actions. These can be led by the people involved in the process too because action research is embedded in what you're doing, it's not a remote academic or theoretical exercise. The learning from this is largely qualitative (although quantitative measures will often support these) and can be used to feed back into the overall process.

In effect, what we propose is an action learning process, where we start with a problem and end up with an iterative solution that has been co-created, co-produced and co-evaluated. The learning opportunities exist not only in terms of the problem:

- Did we fix it?
- Have we learned how to do 'x' better or at less cost?

But also in terms of the process:

- What worked/didn't work?
- What might we change next time?
- Were the right people involved? Who was missing?

As we said at the very beginning of this book, every step is the place to learn!

> ❖ Change becomes stale, so continuously innovate or risk becoming the problem.
> ❖ Use agile methods to manage risk and resource efficiency.
> ❖ Failure is part of success and learning comes from it.
> ❖ Active democracies are inherently active learning systems.
> ❖ Keep it all simple: ignite, do, reflect, learn…

Building Resilience, Planning for Failure

Give light, and the darkness will disappear of itself – Desiderius
Erasmus

Resilience is our ability to restore balance, to become better under
pressure. It's how we get back to equilibrium after a problem or crisis
hits and it underpins our ability to survive and thrive in the long term.
We need to build personal resilience. Our communities need to build
resilience and so do our organisations. We talk about active
democracies as being transformative, so this obviously comes with
risks too. Like any open innovation cycle, there is the potential for set-
backs, mistakes and dead-ends. Failure is not bad, it's part of the
learning process but equally, we have to be aware that some risks can
be counter-productive, even destructive. Being able to respond and
bounce back from these is important. At the broader level, resilience is
an important strategy for strong democracy and healthy communities.

Resilience can be defined and broken down in numerous ways, in the
public sector it can include organisational, economic and community
resilience. Resilient Organisations, a New Zealand-based collaboration,
warns us though that every organisation faces its 'own perfect storm'
and that no individual, organisation or community exists in isolation.
This means that many of the factors that affect us and potentially

destabilise us are beyond our direct control.[90] What we can control is how we react when something does happen.

To be resilient is to focus on the future. It's about refusing to get stuck in the problems of the past. Resilience is about adopting an approach that is flexible, allows for fluidity in our thinking, actions and processes and recognises that adversity brings both growth and learning.

And if the key is to restore balance quickly, then let's recognise that we can't do this alone nearly as effectively as we can do it together. When we seek to build networks of support within our communities and organisations we create an implicit promise of mutual help to overcome our difficulties. Don't wait for adversity, tap into these social networks regularly, build mutuality through authentic connections and, when you're in a crisis situation, they'll be there for you.[91]

Resilience fails in the face of mis-used power but it will thrive where there is reciprocity and trust. It requires effort. That's because resilience is about making sure our communities are connected, understanding where the levers and connecters are and how they operate (and how they are used and perceived by others). As Rosabeth Moss Kanter says, "complacency, arrogance and greed crowd out resilience".[92] The exercise of negative power is an impediment to resilience in our democratic system. What embeds resilience are connections, the strength of character of people and organisations and the core values that motivate us to overcome difficulties and resistance.

Resilience thrives on a sense of community manifested through our actions.

---

[90] See: www.resorgs.org.nz/Content/what-is-organisational-resilience.html
[91] Snyder, S. (2013). Why is resilience so hard? HBR Blogs Nov 3
[92] Moss Kanter, R. (2014). Surprises are the new normal. HBR blog Jul 13

This is a model that Newham Council in London follows,[93] they recognise that resilience thrives where there is the local ability to make decisions about our own lives. They do this through Community Hubs, where local councillors and citizens are involved in resolving local issues and building local capacities. This link with council and their local councillors also ensures that communities are connected rather than isolated.

Newham sees a starting point as identifying your own community's assets and understanding which ones citizens engage with most frequently. These can be the new points of engagement – the touch points – where civic, public and local services are connected directly to people. In Newham, they recognised that 80% of people visit supermarkets and 70% their local doctor or health centre. But they also see other locally specific touch points, sub-communities where the place people go might be a hairdresser, a café or a library.

Resilience is about overcoming adversity, yes, but this is inherently a deficit model. We want to turn this into a positive view of our community. One where we see communities as flourishing and what we do is intervene in agile and timely ways to head-off problems, preserve and, better still, enhance what works. Resilience comes from citizens sharing in a common purpose, where collaboration reinforces connection.

As Newham describes it, resilience is

> about networks and relationships. It's about recognising that part of our strength comes from those around us and the community we belong to.

---

[93] Newham Borough Council (2013). Community resilience in Newham.

It's not about getting hung up on our mistakes (risk culture), it's about how we react and what we do when things don't go to plan (resilient culture). If we're flexible and open, receptive to support and other's ideas we can recover much more quickly. Systems that are connected, learning and future focused are inherently more resilient.

Resilient Organisations[94] identify many aspects of resilience, which they group around three core areas:

- Leadership and culture
- Networks
- [Being] change ready

So resilient organisations are:

- Accountable: they take responsibility
- Collaborative: they support others towards common goals
- Motivated: they take positive steps
- Learning: They reflect and apply learning as they go

Whilst resilience is effectively a strategy for overcoming problems it's important to embed these attributes so that they become an automatic response within the ecosystem. So the strategies you need to help you build resilience are the same ones you need to grow active democracy. At its core, active democracy is about resilient communities.

The place to start is to identify and understand your core assets. These are the ones that create real value for people. They aren't necessarily going to be the same assets or services that your internal metrics tell you are important either, these are the assets (public and private) that citizens and stakeholders tell you matter most to them. Once you know them and understand them you can be much more receptive,

---

[94] See: www.resorgs.org.nz

much more purposeful, in how you use them and how you respond when problems arise with them.

Once you understand your assets, try to understand what makes you resilient and what is holding you back holistically. Consider these four practical features of resilient organisations and question where your own levels of understanding and preparedness are:[95]

- They have a meaningful unifying purpose. It's too easy, particularly in large bureaucratic structures, to get lost in the detail and lose sight of the larger purpose because the operational focus is always at the micro-level. Try to draw back from the complexity of everyday service delivery and citizen support and really focus on what it is that you as an organisation can do for your stakeholders – for citizens – then you'll be able to build a culture that embraces rather than repels.
- Invest in the team. This isn't about clichéd teambuilding exercises, this is about valuing, respecting, trusting and empowering everyone you come into contact with.
- Listening and talking authentically is how you start to give a voice to all the people in the ecosystem that aren't heard. This will help you find the good ideas that have been suppressed and are likely to co-create solutions and crowdsource the answers when they needed.
- Timeframes for turnaround are varied and variable so your response must be flexible and dynamic. There are several factors that influence how long it takes to bounce back, ranging from complexity and culture, to people and the organisational structure.

---

[95] Moss Kanter, R (2013). How to turnaround nearly anything, HBR blog, Nov 13

- ❖ Living with rapid change and regular failure means recognising when failure becomes problematic and how restore balance quickly.
- ❖ Resilience is about people, from the leaders down.
- ❖ People and organisations need to be open, accountable and willing to take action.
- ❖ Know your core strengths and your weaknesses, work with them and improve them.

Get to Know Your Audience

Old world democratic engagement goes for the low hanging fruit; the people and stakeholders that you know and are [too] familiar with. They're what we call the 'direct' audience and whilst they matter, focussing too closely on the easy to identify people already close to you leads to problems. One such problem is that government communication all too often resorts to broadcast-mode when it really needs to nuance the message to reach a wider audience.

For us, it's really important to understand who your audience is and to go beyond the 'usual suspects'. A powerful approach we have used is to view them as part of a wider ecosystem. You don't have to be intimate with the whole system (in fact, as we'll see, you can't be!) but by understanding what it looks like, recognising the pathways to engagement and taking a more nuanced approach you can start to engage with groups that were previously excluded from the process or hard to reach.

To do this, start with an audience mapping exercise. Once you've defined the audience, you can go on to identify relationships, who influences who and then to develop appropriate messages and channels to connect with them. Having a strong understanding of your ecosystem means you can be better targeted and more focussed. The audience map model we use works through a visual metaphor of concentric circles that identify our relationships at four levels, working from the centre out:

Direct	People or groups who directly interact with the project/campaign.
Indirect	People or groups who do not directly interact with the project but exercise strong influence over (or are strongly influenced/affected by) direct users.
Remote	People or groups who remain at a distance from the project but could be affected/influenced by the project (or vice versa, could indirectly affect/influence).
Societal	Wider societal influences. Usually macro, they have no direct impact or influence and are themselves either not affected by or very indirectly affected by the system. This might include legislators or local authorities, quality assurance agencies or professional governing bodies and typical refers to a macro-level change or rule, law or policy has a trickle-down impact on this project.

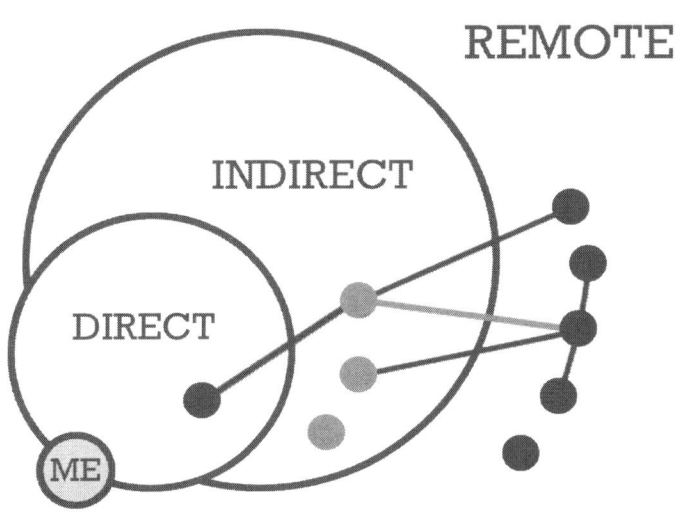

To get started, draw an Audience Map outline on a whiteboard, an electronic template or on big sheets of paper. Just so long as everyone can see it clearly and there's plenty of room for writing! Some simple rules for a successful mapping session are:

- Don't just aim for the obvious and try and push the boundaries! Consider what disagreement might occur as to the roles and relative influence of others. We will all approach this exercise form different points of view.
- Don't dismiss difference, let it evolve through discussion and move towards consensus. Lack of awareness, limited exposure to a wider audience or failing to legitimate the role of people or groups for political or power reasons all lead to different weightings. But when this audience mapping exercise is carried out amongst a broad group it can lead to a more accurate, neutral and more widely accepted definition of your relationships, influences and influencers. It is also more likely to inform the group's own knowledge.
- Don't let one person, or one way of thinking about the eco-system influence the outcome – stay open to new and diverse views of your world!
- And try not to uncritically copy down lists of stakeholders that you already have, these are OK to use as a reminder but this will work better if it's a living map of your real world.

Ask the people in your group to suggest stakeholders and then nominate where they belong. Stakeholders can be people, organisations, media, in fact, anyone! Sometimes they can even be intangible objects too, such as Acts of Parliament, because they are a key influence on what you do (or you need to get one changed to succeed). At this stage, it can work well to take a brainstorming approach. You don't need to question or challenge where things go and there's plenty of time later to refine the map.

You can focus on one category at a time or just add the names as they come up. It is often easier to start with the "direct" stakeholders as they tend to be the more obvious and more readily drawn to mind because people are aware of who they are already – although there might be a few surprises by the time you've finished. This can act as a helpful warm-up for the rest of the process too.

As you work out through the circles, it can become increasingly challenging for the group to identify the audience. The brainstorming phase tends to last between 10 and 15 minutes but could be more depending on the nature of the group and the complexity of the project or campaign. Obviously, mapping stakeholders for the whole organisation is going to take you longer than for a small project.

Once you've reached what feels like saturation point and no more new stakeholders are coming up, you should end up with a model that looks something like the one over the page. Now you can start to refine the map!

Ask the group to work through the stakeholders and confirm that they are happy with where they've been put. You're aiming for some reasonable group consensus here and, given that this model is always subjective, this shared understanding can be more important than absolute accuracy. Work from the centre outwards and, where there is disagreement, create the space for the group to explore and discuss. You can also use this phase to merge entries and remove any duplication.

This is not meant to be exhaustive, just to give you a shared understanding of your stakeholders before you start making assumptions about what it is that you're doing, the impact that it will have and how to engage with them.

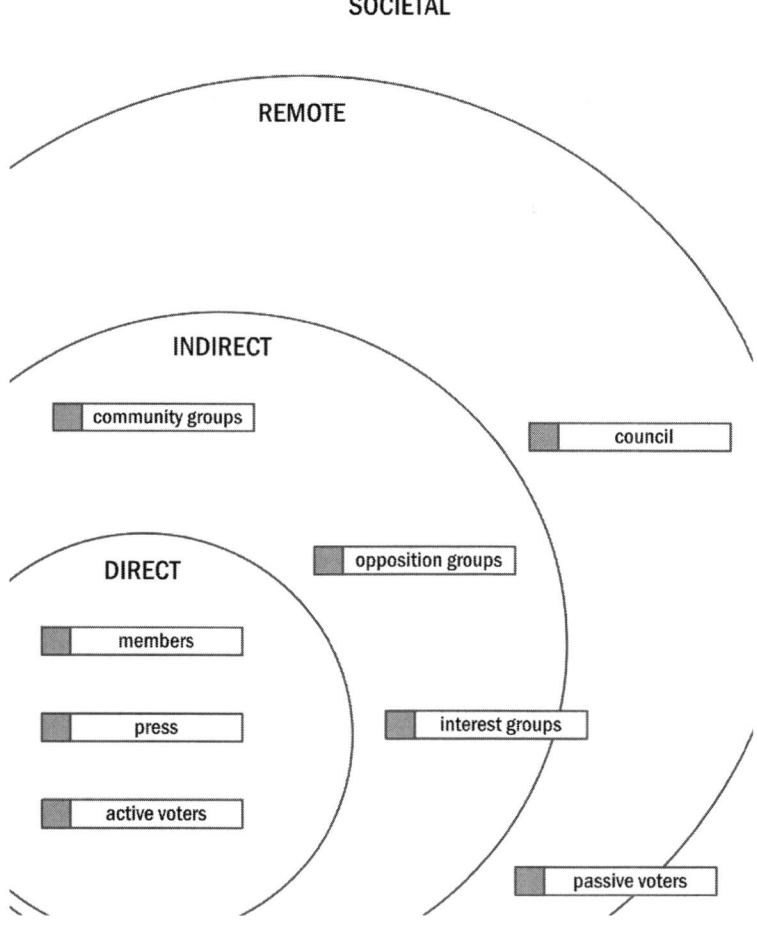

SOCIETAL

REMOTE

INDIRECT

community groups

council

DIRECT

opposition groups

members

press

interest groups

active voters

passive voters

Now that you have a list of stakeholders in the right place, identifying the relationships that exist between them can significantly help you to understand your stakeholder ecosystem. Primary relationships can usually be found to exist between stakeholders in neighbouring circles and within circles (especially the innermost "direct" group). You can describe the relationship that exists (and the direction it flows) on the diagram if you wish (this will help you understand influence and the

effect of communication and information across the eco-system).
Taking a portion of the example from earlier, we can add some
relationships and describe the nature of those relationships too:

- Press *informs* Active voters
- Active voters *influence* Passive voters
- Press *informs* Passive voters

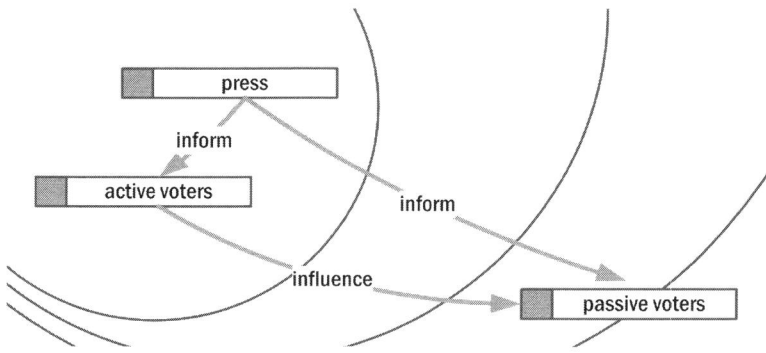

What we learn from this example is that two groups of people who are
actively connected to what we are doing (i.e. in a direct relationship
with our campaign or project), in this case the press and active voters,
are able to connect to a remote group of stakeholders that we are
unlikely to be able to exert any significance over, namely passive
voters. Once you get to know your stakeholders – your audience – and
how strongly they affect/influence or are affected/influenced by the
project or campaign, you've also gained some understanding of the
key relationships that exist between stakeholders (and between you
and the stakeholders).

The end-result of this process is a graphical representation of the
stakeholder ecosystem in the form of an Audience Map. This shows not
only where you can directly influence but how you can reach those
hard to reach groups by working with third-parties and by allowing

them to become channels for your engagement. Here's our earlier example again, this time with the relationships added in. This is your completed Audience Map. A useful place to begin before you start making assumptions about what it is that you're doing and the impact that it will have.

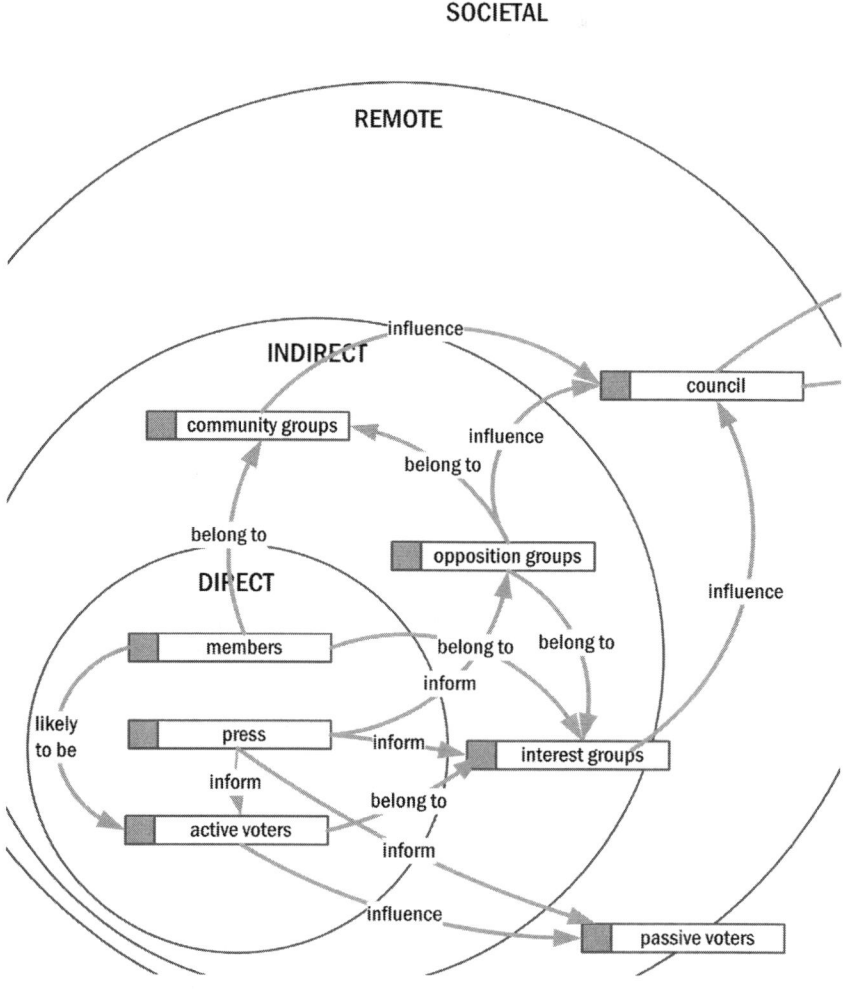

- ❖ Understand who your real audience going beyond those close to you.
- ❖ Look for partners and pathways to connect more widely.
- ❖ Trust your network with the message and give them the power to re-shape it for their own audiences.
- ❖ Recognise the dynamics and relationships in your audience ecosystem.

Understanding Influence and Value

A visual representation like the audience map helps to build awareness and a shared understanding of all the actors and agencies involved in a place or project. The next stage is to understand how these groups relate and inter-relate. Understanding this will help you develop strategies for connecting, listening, communicating and engaging beyond the broad-brush models of traditional government communication. This example uses a sub-set of the Audience Map from the previous chapter to explore influence and value:

STAKEHOLDER	INFLUENCES/ AFFECTS	INFLUENCED/ AFFECTED BY	DESCRIPTION OF ROLE
DIRECT			
Party members	Other members Active voters Interest groups	Active voters Press Interest groups	Party members are the key project workers for the campaign. At this level of granularity, it includes candidates.
Active voters	Party members Passive voters Interest groups	Press Party members	This describes the section of the community who are actively informed regarding local body politics.

You can see from this that relationships can exist one or both ways and that a single stakeholder can be both influenced and an influencer. Often you will see that complex circular relationships exist. Influence moves outwards through the layers of the Audience Map only to return to the centre through the influence of other groups.

Influence can be obvious or subtle but not understanding who influences who else in your eco-system risks focusing time and effort in the wrong place. Spend some time looking at the key stakeholders on your Audience Map (most likely those in your direct sphere but it could include others further out if they are critically important) and how they are related to you and to others.

Ask yourself:

- Where do they get their information from?
- Who are they closely aligned with?
- Who do they trust?
- What is the value exchange between you and your key stakeholders?

You might then want to describe these interfaces and interactions:

ORGANI-SATION	INFLUENCES	INFLUENCED	VALUE FOR THEM	VALUE FOR US
Interest Group A	Party, Public, Media	Parliamentary party, International organisations	Support, credibility, policy expertise	Voice in council

In the hierarchical world of arrogant democracy, you can really only ever understand enough about the direct audience to be able to shape a message for them. Anything further out was just a blur. You now have a good understanding of the people and organisations in your audience eco-system, how they relate to each other and their relationship with yourself and others. Specifically, you understand their distance from you and their level of influence and importance in the wider eco-system.

It's now possible to define and categorise your audience and to understand where it's useful and constructive to direct your energy, who needs more work and which groups might remain too hard for you to engage directly with (in which case, consider how indirect channels via others in your audience ecosystem can be used to bridge the gap). Think about the people you want to target for engagement. Whether it's creating a call to action to make your theory of change real for people, influencing their thinking and decision making or targeting some kind of behaviour change, you can now focus on developing your campaign messages according to each stakeholder's level of interest and influence:

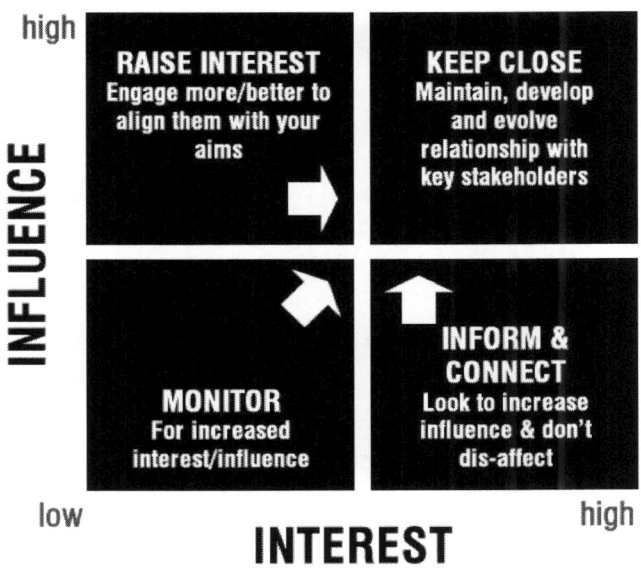

- **Monitor** those with low interest and low levels of influence.
- **Inform and connect** with those in your audience who have a high interest in what you are doing, but exhibit relatively low levels of influence. This group matter because they can be supported to become more influential (by you and others, particularly through social media) and they are also potentially able to become dis-engaged and dis-affected and therefore become negative influencers.
- **Maintain interest** from those who are key influencers but have lower levels of interest (examples include politicians and journalists). You need to ensure that this group is kept connected to your campaign. Consider too that you want to encourage them to become more informed and more positively engaged but there is also a risk of them becoming dis-affected.
- **Keep close** to the key influencers with high levels of knowledge and expertise. These are the critical influencers in your network and must always be a focus of any communications strategy. It is too easy to focus on shifting other groups towards your position at the expense of maintaining the relationship and message with those already close.
- It is critically important that your communications strategy incorporates **reflection and listening**, particularly with the latter two groups.

Here's an example of the influence and interest matrix using our earlier example. You'll see that one of these stakeholders exerts potentially strong negative influence – make sure to include any opposition within your eco-system and be aware of its impact so you can develop counter-strategies):

		Low	High
INFLUENCE	High	Press Community groups	Members Interest groups Opposition (-ve)
	Low	Passive voters Council	Active voters
		Low	High

INTEREST

You can map the stakeholders you identified earlier across the four quadrants above and then ask these questions:

- What do they think now? → **Beliefs**
- What do we want them to think? → **Change**
- What do we want them to say when they talk about us? → **Narrative**
- What do you want them to do to make this change happen? → **Action**

You now have a starting point (as is) and a tangible end point (where to). The challenge is to create an action plan for each key stakeholder (or groups of stakeholders where this is appropriate – but remember that the broader the audience the more generic the message and you might lose some of the necessary nuancing in your message).

WHO	WHAT THEY THINK	WE WANT THEM TO THINK	WE WANT THEM TO SAY	WHAT WE HAVE TO DO
Press	No track record	They might be new together but individually they're hugely experienced	Experience comes together to bring a new refreshing face to local politics: Better together	Promote established candidates Point to track record Create inspiring electoral ticket
	Single issue party	One issues might be a catalyst for formation but the track record goes right across all the key issues	Recognise all the important issues	Ensure that policies are clearly promoted Show range of previous successes
	Not interested because new	They're Strong, serious contenders: a credible force	An interesting and viable new force *who can win*	Track record combined with strong local candidates and clear message. Engage in public debate

For each of your target audience, you might also want to consider:

- Their direct and indirect influencers (who do they listen to)
- Their values
- Potential triggers for change
- Favoured and appropriate methods and media for communication

You know who matters, what they think and what you need to do to get them to support you (or to counter what they say if they are counter-positional). Now is the time to activate your campaign or communications strategy. One very simple model we suggest you can use for this is:

- Message; Momentum; and Mass

It's rarely productive to simply argue that something is wrong. People want solutions, not more problems. So all that does is place you on one side of what is already likely to be a polarised debate. To overcome this we recommend a simple three-part story:

- Explain the problem your campaign or product will solve.
- Make the story personal, relevant and compelling.
- Be clear about what you want to people to do (don't leave them guessing).

In other words, create an outcome focussed, human-level call to action! If you're a charity, chances are you're already good at this. Yet often this is exactly what our elected representatives are missing and need to hear. In a world of evidence-based policy, it's even more important to relate the campaign to something real and human because people will engage emotionally with this as well as logically with the underlying data. This is a key to turning advocacy into a compelling case. A drop of water eventually becomes an ocean and the chances are that you are not alone.

The next stage is to create momentum. You know who the key influencers are and you've worked out how to reach them, look for the network multipliers and ensure that you're not just one voice shouting in a crowd.

The third stage is to consider whether you need to create mass. Some campaigns need mass public engagement, such as where online campaigning can significantly raise the attention around an issue.

Others may need strategic partnerships with one or two relevant organisations to add clout. You need to think hard around this, as there is no right answer and no checkbox answer. Sometimes both are needed. Either way, it pays to think open and collaboratively around campaigns, especially where others can bring something unique to the table, add credibility or help spread the message. Unusual partnerships can show strength and depth, both of which can be valued by policy makers and lawmakers.

There's power in these numbers. But once the campaign has got going it is all about getting in front of the people that matter – the decision-makers. By all means use the mass-email technique to raise your profile and demonstrate support but alone it's as likely to frustrate lawmakers as it is to engage them. Back up your story with policy by explaining what's happening, the impact if it happens and what should happen instead.

- ❖ Really understand who has influence.
- ❖ Get to know the key information pathways in your network.
- ❖ Develop messages based on people's interest and engagement, not your own.
- ❖ Avoid assumptions about homogeneity.
- ❖ It's about message, momentum and mass.

Frame Your Campaign

Think about election posters, debates and party political broadcasts. Think about how the sudden onset of summer brings out endless TV commercials trying to sell us garden furniture or how charities try to persuade us to sign up to a good cause. These are all campaigns and if you want to advance the principles of active democracy and build momentum for the democratic movement (and indeed make good democracy work in a practical and real way) there are things that you can learn from them.

A campaign is just a project. Like all projects it has a beginning (planning), a middle (execution) and an end (evaluation). Like all good campaigns you need a call to action, you're asking people to do something! In this case it's get engaged, understand the situation better and take part in the conversation: it's help co-design their own futures!

There are many books written about campaigning and we don't intend to re-invent the wheel here, so what we're going to say at this stage is get to know campaigning methods and see how they can help you. Whether you're trying to engage a sceptical public or create change within your organisation, elements of good campaign planning can help you.

Our simple model for a clear campaign structure is based on six key stages.

Target

Define concrete outcomes: this is was what we will achieve by the end of the project. Make it realistic but equally have some ambition when setting targets.

Measure

Make these outcomes measurable so that you know you're going in the right direction and whether you succeeded (or not). Spend some time defining the metrics you want to record but make sure they are realistic, for example, the number of signatures on a petition is one measure that's often used but did people simply sign and walk away (indicating support but little engagement) or did they actually mobilise and take action, become part of the campaign? Think about how the metrics that matter change during the lifecycle of the campaign too.

Focus

Answer the following questions to make sure that your campaign has focus and keep checking back to see if they hold true or are changing to ensure that your focus is in the right place:

- Who is your audience?
- What does your audience want to hear?
- What do you want that audience to do?
- How would you like your audience to scale the campaign and own the message?
- What are your priorities?

Actions

Consider direct actions that you can take to build momentum and mass as well as how you support others to create indirect momentum for you. Remember we're about co-creating so we also want you to think about how you co-create campaigns and let go of the message so people in your indirect and remote audiences can hear your message in their voice from people closer to them that they trust.

Fine tune
Constantly reflect on what is happening and be prepared to change the message, pivot the campaign and refine the metrics, use the 'backcasting' model we described earlier as a way of doing and containing this.

Close
No, you're not finished yet, sorry! It doesn't matter how it went, good or bad, it's also about learning from the process. Evaluate what worked and what didn't work, what you could do differently and what you would do again. Really get to understand what happened and you will be better equipped next time.

❖ Maximise the impact of your campaigns by knowing who to target, when and with what message.

❖ Campaigns aren't magic, they're just another project.

❖ Ensure that you create a meaningful call to action so people who engage know what to do next.

❖ Measure, learn, reflect and refine.

Politics Needs to Change Itself

This book is about changing democracy for the better. We've focussed our conversations on the systems of governance and engagement; how to make these better, more responsive and more like the world we live in. How to get more of us to help make democracy work better for more of us. To us, democracy is about much more than elections, the critical stuff is what happens between them. But modern democracy is made up of citizens, officials *and* elected representatives. So we feel that we have to highlight the responsibility to change the way politics works too as part of the move to active democracies. Change is personal, it cannot be imposed as this creates resistance. Hence for politics and politicians to change, they must want this change for themselves. We meet politicians on a daily basis in our work, we regularly come into contact with incredible people who are really in touch and ready to create meaningful actions with the people around them. However, we also meet far too much arrogance, elitism and a sense of superiority. In these cases, their 'insideness' is more of a problem than their 'outsideness'.

Democracy and politics are nervously, sometimes awkwardly, but always critically, inter-twined. Public dis-satisfaction with democracy all too often turns out to be dis-affection with politics (and politicians). The public has a particular dislike for the nasty, manipulative, macho and patriarchal old world politics that is all too visible in the media and parliamentary chambers. Politicians appear to so many of us to be out of touch, to have lost any understanding or empathy for the lives of 'ordinary' people. And this could be because, as Jennifer Lees-

Marshment observes, in many ways, they are out of touch with some parts of the democratic system. She suggests that our politicians fail to hear what is being said because:[96]

1.   Politicians are not involved in the public input system
2.   Politicians don't see the potential benefit of public input
3.   Most public input is unusable for politicians
4.   The nature and realities of government hinder integration of public input
5.   Politicians are there to make the final decision in a pragmatic sense
6.   Public input systems don't make space for political leadership
7.   Public input raises questions for the traditional representative role of politicians

Active politics is a subject in its own right and one we were tempted to leave alone. Why? Because we don't want you to feel that politics is the core focus of democracy. People should be. Good governance should be. All too often politics is the problem. And as soon as one introduces the subject of politics, people take sides, start looking for biases in our argument and then build their argument around what they already believe in. Rather than engage in a real conversation, they take sides and become defensive. And we need more real conversations. But we feel that, briefly at least, this is a risk we'll have to take.

As we're writing this we have just had the 2014 elections to the European Parliament. Right across Europe we have seen a seismic shift in the public's attitudes to incumbency. Right across Europe we have seen long established political elites shaken out of their complacency with a vote against them. Not in many cases a vote for something, most often a vote against. A vote against arrogance. A vote against the misuse of power and control. The British media naturally focussed on

---

[96] Lees-Marshment, J. (2014). The Ministry of Public Input: Report and recommendations for practice. Auckland: University of Auckland. p.7

the rise of the right-leaning UK Independence Party. UKIP's rise is not entirely one of grassroots alternative politics, it's a well-funded, carefully orchestrated campaign of faux-populism that the media has bought into. But elsewhere and more broadly the story of Europe 2014 denies the naïve narratives of old-world left/right polarisation, instead marking a turning of popular support away from the status quo. The public have already turned away from membership of the 'established' political parties. Now voters are angry. They are turning away from the people whom many believe have orchestrated and manipulated the systems of governance. Many of us believe that power is used, not for the good of the many, but for the benefit of the few. And there is strong evidence to suggest we are right.[97]

Our challenge now is can we harness this power-shift to grow, mature and deliver a new kind of politics to support a new kind of democracy? Can we build an active politics that moves towards deliberation, inclusion and co-creation?

A good reason to keep politics away from democracy is that, all too often, it has little to do with it. Politics in 21st Century Europe (and elsewhere) is more about economics, more about protecting power and growing private wealth than it is about building a democratic, inclusive or fair society. Then again, perhaps that's the very reason we need to mention it here. Just as neo-liberalism colonises the language of democracy, trying to make us 'consumers' not citizens, so it does the same with politics, insidiously arguing that good democratic governance is more akin to corporate governance and can only be trusted to an elite. Arguing that the good stewards of our society are the ones who balance the budgets (though curiously they have failed to manage this), rather than those who care about our children, elderly or infirm. That bankers deserve eye-watering bonuses because

---

[97] Hager, N. (2014). Dirty politics: How attack politics is poisoning New Zealand's political environment. Nelson: Craig Potton Publishing; Jones, O. (2014). The Establishment: And how they get away with it. London: Penguin.

198
Road Map for Active Democracies

it's market forces' whilst the poorest 40% in Britain fall further into debt year-upon-year.[98]

The challenge is also one against technocracy. Whether it is southern Europe's anger at the social and economic havoc resulting from fiscal bailouts or the increasing scepticism and dislike for the heavy-laden bureaucracy of Brussels, reflected in votes in Sweden, Denmark and the Netherlands, as well more obviously in the UK and France.

It is telling that, in the work we do, we work with many in government who are receptive to change but they frustrated by what they see as a growing resistance from politicians. Politicians who appear to be becoming more entrenched and controlling, despite the shift in the public mood towards openness. In the different countries we visit we regularly hear that despite talk of open government and transparency politicians are more and more trying to close down debate and cement their own personal power. But as we've said in this book, personal power used in this way ultimately fails and hopefully what we are seeing in Europe in 2014 are the first cracks in this failure of power.

This gives us more reason than ever to co-create new active democracies that are fit for the future. But also more reason than ever to do so in thoughtful ways. As we've already argued, positive change cannot step into a void but needs a carefully curated transition or it will fail. It needs political buy-in as well as the civic and technical.

The time is not just right it is overdue not just to re-design our systems of democracy but also the methods by which we select, elect and hold to account the people who govern us. Some people talk of digital democracies and new deliberative formats of democracy, where representatives are replaced by collective decision making. To be

---

[98] Meyer, H. (2014, May 29). UK's richest can save £18,680 a year as poorest 40% spend more than they earn. The Guardian: theguardian.com/uk-news/2014/may/29/richest-uk-save-poorest-spend-crisis-post-office-data

honest, we feel that in reality this is a step too far, at least for now. Though new digital tools certainly will help, representation in some form or other seems logically necessary for the foreseeable future. Given the imbalance in power and control, moving to a fully deliberative model would simply replace one elite with another, and the majority of the population would remain just as disengaged as ever. But alternatives to the big political parties are emerging everywhere! From the Pirate Parties in Iceland, Germany and Sweden, to emergent citizens' movements, such as Podemos in Spain. We're even seeing successful examples of groups of independent non-aligned politicians coming together at the local government level in the UK, such as the 'Independents for Frome' movement described in the book 'Flatpack Democracy'.[99]

Whilst we've tried to avoid politics, the reality is that we cannot reform democracy without reforming politics too. But politics can only reform itself if it recognises that its insider-status is a problem and is able to see its own relative and co-participatory place in the democratic ecosystem. If active democracies are to work for everyone then we need a new form of active politics that is open, inclusive and collaborative, that recognises difference and challenges oppression and hatred. A form of politics that is part of the networked ecosystem of new active democracies. Talking about the 2014 European Parliamentary Elections, a UK-based social think tank said,

> the election result makes the case for a new politics overwhelming. The future can neither be denied nor avoided. The world is changing – we either bend it to us, to build a good society, or we will be forced to bend to it. [100]

---

[99] Macfadyen, P. (2014). Flatpack democracy. Eco-logic Books: Bath
[100] See: www.compassonline.org.uk/post-election-statement-leaving-the-20th-century

For us, the most obvious pathway is to improve both the quality and quantity of systems that we have so that they are more relevant, accessible and appealing to the public, for example, when it comes to the electoral process:

1. Ensure fairer systems for selecting our representatives, such as using open primaries to compensate for falling party membership.
2. Ensure that electoral systems are fully proportional (a particular problem in the UK), this can help to negate adversarial politics so that more people feel represented and to limit the bi-polar dominance of big parties.
3. Enable more flexible ways of voting, ranging from online, mobile, in person and postal and lengthen the voting periods for some of these methods so that voting can take place over a period of days.
4. Limit party funding and third-party campaigning to ensure that well-funded interest groups cannot manipulate elections as they do at present and to ensure that power and incumbency do not magnify into electoral advantage.
5. Enforce transparency in campaigning and campaign funding.

Once the election's over we need to:

1. Enshrine open government and transparency in all public activities so that governments are open by default, not exception.
2. Encourage innovative forms of representation so that politicians are required to be engaged and conversational. Methods such as liquid democracy[101], participatory decision making and referendums can all be used, though none is itself

---

[101] Liquid Democracy is the combination of networks and democracy where votes flow through networks of trusted relationships using methods of delegation. See: liquiddemocracy.org

a panacea and the underlying processes must be right or they are simply placebos.

3. Encourage third parties to hold representatives to account through formats such as citizen journalism and by ensuring that democracy is always open and citizens have the right to attend, report on and even broadcast the proceedings of their representatives.
4. Give citizens the power of recall over their representatives so that those who do not act appropriately or as they promised can be sacked.
5. Promote information and political literacy so that the public is more able to see through manipulation and recognise bias in their information sources.

Above all, we argue, we need to apply the precepts of active democracies that we've described in this book not just to the policy development, decision making and service delivery aspects of government but also to the representative process. We want to harness new technologies and the passion that currently goes untapped, breaking down the barriers of old world politics to get people back in touch with democracy.

❖ Like it or not, politics is a key part of democracy and we need to change this too.

❖ Politics has become too much about economics and protecting narrow interests.

❖ Politics can only reform itself if it recognises that its insider-status is a problem.

❖ Political systems need to see themselves as relative and co-participatory places in the democratic ecosystem.

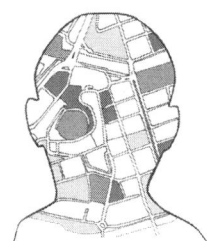

Invitation to Co-creation

Join us in the Conversation

We believe that democracy has to change. If you didn't before, we hope you do now. And we hope that you share at least some of our sense of urgency. We believe that it's time to create new models of democracy, models that are ready for the future. We think that what's needed are models that remain agile and responsive to our changing needs. Above all, we need democracies that encourage and embrace participation from as many people as want to get involved (and we hope that's everyone, because democracy affects all of us).

Through this book we've tried to present our thoughts on the problems we face. We've attempted to bring together some ideas that we feel can change our democracies for the better. We've tried not to be prescriptive or offer monolithic solutions. We've said it already, but democracy is not a 'one size fits all' thing. What we hope we've done is introduce you to some ideas and concepts that can support the transformation you need. Back at the beginning, when we were laying out our reasons for writing this book, we gave you four principles that guide our work, these were:

- control is over-rated;
- power used to create personal advantage will always fail;
- crowds are better at creating the future; and
- self-reflection helps us understand the impact of our actions.

We hope that these have permeated through the book and that, used well, the suggestions we have made will help us all to overcome the negatives and strengthen the positives that we encounter so that our new networked, active democracies work in ways that ensure:

- uncertainty is embraced;
- power is shared;
- openness, co-creation and co-production are default methods; and
- we practice active learning.

The old ways don't work, so we need new solutions. We hope that this book can be a catalyst for this new thinking, for new forms of leadership and new ways to design and deliver democracy and public services.

We want to leave behind the old, tired ways of arrogance and control and embrace instead democratic intimacy and co-creation. The future, we believe, will be created together. The journey is going to be challenging, it will be resisted, but the level of change and uncertainty we have in the world today leaves us with no choice. We have to re-invent democracy and we all have a right to be part of the process.

If we are to reflect on what this means for our democratic ecosystems, we hope to find them reconstructing themselves to look more like the picture overleaf.

We also said at the beginning that this book is more than a simple text, it's an invitation. An invitation for you and anyone else who believes in active democracies to get involved. We don't believe we have the answers, we certainly can't tell you what your destination is. All we've been able to do, we hope, is equip you for some of the journey. The solutions we need to develop lie in the collective mind, not just ours.

That's why we want you to become a partner and even to consider becoming a co-author in our project. We want you to join in the conversation with us. We want to encourage you take what we've written and use it to help transform your own democracy.

This isn't the last word, it's the start of a conversation, so we would like to invite you to join the conversation...

Co-create with us!
For information on how to get involved,
workshops, facilitation and bespoke training,
join us at: activedemocraci.es

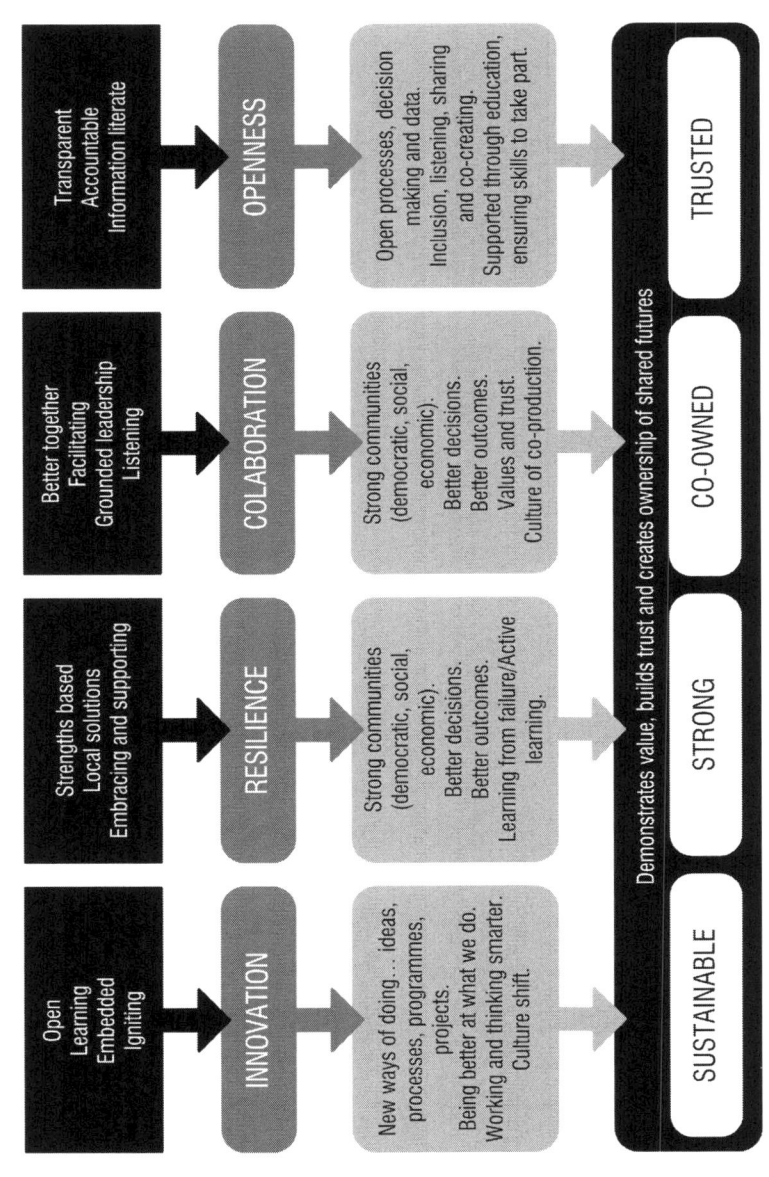

Invitation to Co-creation

About the Authors

Andy Williamson

Andy works globally to transform democratic leadership and engagement across parliaments, governments and civil society. Through facilitation, critical thinking, creativity and innovation he finds new ways to engage the public in democracy and helps to transform how organisations think, function and collaborate. A New Zealander based in the UK, he was Director of Digital Democracy at the Hansard Society before founding Democratise (democrati.se) in 2012. Andy is a Fellow of the RSA, the Chair of Do-It UK and a Governor of the Democratic Society. He holds a PhD from Monash University, Australia and is a published poet. Find him on Twitter at @andy_williamson or at andywilliamson.com.

Martin Sande

Martin is a creative thinker and facilitator based in Gothenburg, Sweden. Using dialogue, conflict resolution and facilitation skills, his work involves leaders in shared learning and capacity building so they can thrive in complexity, creating more resilient people, organisations and societies. Martin, often described as an "energy field of opportunity and mind shifting thinking and practice", leads Co-lab by Preera, an innovation lab for learning and enabling practices for meeting complexity. It is based within Preera, a Swedish management consultancy and founding member of the Transformation Alliance. Find him on Twitter at @martinsande.

Index